FOLK MUSIC OF HUNGARY

ZOLTÁN KODÁLY

FOLK MUSIC
OF HUNGARY

Enlarged edition revised by Lajos Vargyas

Translated by Ronald Tempest and Cynthia Jolly

Translation revised by Laurence Picken

PRAEGER PUBLISHERS
New York · Washington

BOOKS THAT MATTER

Published in the United States of America in 1971
by Praeger Publishers, Inc.,
111 Fourth Avenue, New York, N. Y. 10003

Hungarian edition, A MAGYAR NÉPZENE, published in 1952 by
Zeneműkiadó Vállalat, Budapest, Hungary

Translated from the Hungarian and revised in accordance with
the German edition (1956) by Ronald Tempest and Cynthia Jolly
Jacket and binding by Erika Urai

First English edition published in 1960 by Barrie and Rockliff
(Barrie Books Ltd.), 2 Clement's Inn, Strand, London WC 2

Library of Congress Catalog Card Number: 75-125391
Printed and bound in Hungary

AUTHOR'S PREFACE TO THE ENGLISH EDITION

It is with pleasure that I offer this book to English readers, in the hope of supplying them with ample information about Hungarian folk music.

Interest in the subject has never been lacking. Dame Sybil Thorndike, when interviewed once about my music, instantly mentioned a song from Francis Korbay's *Hungarian Melodies*—it was undoubtedly the similarity of our names that caused the confusion. Unfortunately, Korbay's very popular volume contains hardly a single genuine folksong, and the same applies to other popular publications.

Folk music was similarly absent from the repertory of famous town gipsy bands. Only during the last few decades, stimulated by the Hungarian Radio, did they begin gradually to learn traditional peasant tunes, the accompaniment of which still consists too often of inappropriate harmonies derived from their hackneyed routine.

Bartók's book *Hungarian Folk Music* (Oxford University Press, 1931) provided thorough information for those interested. Unfortunately, Bartók's study only reached a small circle of experts—the public scarcely at all. Generally speaking, Hungarian folk music is still identified with gipsy music, and folksong is confused with popular art-music. Yet in its narrower sense, Hungarian folk music has little or nothing in common with the music offered over the radio as 'Hungarian folk tunes' or, since Sarasate, as 'gipsy melodies.' Performed by gipsy orchestras or in other popular arrangements, such music has been the basis of all generalizations about 'Hungarian music' for nearly a hundred years. Nor is it in any way the creation of gipsies, as still frequently asserted owing to Franz Liszt's monumental error.

It is generally possible to identify the composers of the various tunes, that include the themes of Brahms's *Hungarian Dances* and Liszt's *Hungarian Rhapsodies*. They all lived in the nineteenth century, and the most outstanding were Hungarians of noble descent. To mention but a few: Kálmán Simonffy of Marosvásárhely (1832–1889), Elemér Szentirmay, whose real name was János Németh of Zsid and Vadasfa (1836–1908); Béni Egressy, whose full name was Benjámin Galambos of Egres (1814–1851). Others came from bourgeois families that had been assimilated, such as Béla Kéler (1820–1882) and Károly Thern (1817–1886), both from the Szepes region which, from the twelfth century onwards, was settled by Germans. Of countless gipsy musicians very few were composers: Miska Farkas (1829–1890) and Pál Rácz (1837–1886).

The gipsy contribution was not very distinguished, with the possible exception of Pista Dankó (1858–1903); his compositions evidently postdate Liszt, since Liszt's *Des Bohémiens et de leur musique en Hongrie* appeared in 1859.

A number of songs, written by still unidentified composers, show by their style that they too belong to this period.

Although text and melody were sometimes written by the same person, the harmonic accompaniment was generally written by another, as happened with polyphonic sixteenth-century *chansons* and the minnesingers' *Töne*.

The Hungarian composers mentioned above were nearly always inexperienced amateurs. The tunes became common property soon after their appearance, and nobody inquired after their origin. Despite the Copyright Law of 1886, everything was freely reprinted until, with the beginning of the twentieth century, the modern idea of author's rights came into existence.

Hence in its essentials the style of Hungarian popular music, as generally known, was formed in the middle of the nineteenth century. Its rhythmical characteristics spring from language and dance; its tunes were a later outcrop of an older type in which Western European influences are traceable. A single feature, the so-called 'gipsy scale,' points to a Southern Oriental (Arabic) origin, and may possibly have reached Hungary through the gipsies:

I.

Gipsies falsify the folksongs they play by introducing the augmented intervals of this scale, which are rarely used by peasants. It should be emphasized, however, that the gipsy scale by no means predominates in gipsy style and that modern major and minor scales are much more frequent.

Gipsy composers followed faithfully in the footsteps of other native and assimilated Hungarians. The most prolific, Pista Dankó, was quite strongly under the influence of indigenous Hungarian peasant music. He wrote more than four hundred songs to contemporary Hungarian texts, whereas other gipsy composers confined themselves to the wordless, and instrumentally conceived, *csárdás*.

This is not to say that real gipsy music does not exist; it consists of short songs in Romany, known and sung today, mainly by nomadic 'tent-colonies' and to a lesser extent by settled village gipsies; the civilized town-gipsies, and hence the musicians, do not know them at all. Still largely unexplored territory, these songs have virtually nothing in common with the Hungarian popular style or with true Hungarian folksong. A more thoroughgoing stylistic analysis may some day make it possible to trace the origins of certain features in gipsy compositions; but gipsy composers at best are never more than second-rate imitators of the true Hungarian style.

In recent decades there has been a revival of the gipsy style which has assumed at least quantitative importance. The chief exponents are again native Hungarians such as Lóránd Fráter of Ipp and Érkeserű (1872–1923) and Árpád Balázs (1874–1941), or assimilated Hungarians such as Ernő Lányi (1861–1923). There is a conspicuous absence of gipsy composers today.

It is entirely erroneous, therefore, to regard the music played by gipsies from about 1850 onwards as 'gipsy music.' It is quite clear that most of the pieces were (and still are) written, not by gipsies but by Hungarians, and any gipsies concerned have taken over a style created by others. In origin and character this style belonged to the town tradition of printed art-music, and had nothing to do with 'ancient tradition' or the like. True, it spread by word of mouth; gipsies performed it without written music, and it was sung by large numbers of musically illiterate people. It was assimilated by the average Hungarian, and more especially by the town-dweller, although a great deal of it also found its way into the villages. Superficial observers may be forgiven for having fallen into the trap of thinking that it was typical folksong.

The following example by Elemér Szentirmay has become world-famous. It is the main theme of Sarasate's *Gipsy Melodies*, in which it appears in a corrupt form. Compare the following original notation:

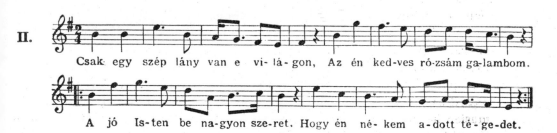

II. Csak egy szép lány van e vi-lá-gon, Az én ked-ves ró-zsám ga-lambom.

A jó Is-ten be na-gyon sze-ret. Hogy én né-kem a-dott té-ge-det.

A comparison of this tune with Schubert's *Serenade* illustrates how this style was formed under the influence of West European melodies. It is undeniably Hungarian in essence, but its Western trappings may explain its vast popularity outside Hungary.

The genuine old folk-tradition is not visible even in the musical style that immediately preceded this, the style that flourished in Hungary during the first half of the nineteenth century. It too was town art-music, in essence nothing but dance music; at first it was even written by foreigners and immigrants, and, like its later counterpart, was to be found in print.

The first *Danses Hongroises*—sometimes just called *Hongroises*—were composed by men with names such as Bengraf, Franz Tost, Drechsler, Mohaupt, Stocker. It is still a mystery where they obtained the Hungarian trimmings for their mediocre pieces, formed and harmonized in the Viennese style. A few copies of anonymous dances of that period, published in Vienna, and including the source of Haydn's 'Rondo all'ongarese,' show traces of an earlier, more primitive, instrumental tradition. This may have survived among gipsy musicians of the day, since scattered traces of it still remain in remote villages.

Later music in this style was provided by János Lavotta of Izsépfalva and Kevelháza (1763–1820), János Svastits of Bocsár (c. 1800–1874), the Vice-Paladin Kázmér of Sárköz (1799–1876), and the physician J. B. of Hunyad (1807–1865)—all Hungarians—and also by the Czech Anton Csermák (1807–1865), self-styled Baronet of Dlujk and Rouhans, the gipsy János Bihari (1764–1827), and a Jew, Márk Rózsavölgyi (1789–1848), whose death inspired Petőfi's famous, deeply-felt poem. Newly-awakened national feeling swept aside differences of birth and background: in the service of 'national music' all found themselves on common ground.

Most of this music now seems old-fashioned and dated; only the compositions of Bihari still teem with life. But since he had no knowledge of musical notation, there will never be any certainty about what is his, and what has been added by those who noted down and copied his music. At all events, several of his pieces are related to traditional Hungarian peasant music. He forms the only link between the peasant tradition and the urban dance music that produced the *csárdás* round about 1830.

The intention of the present work is to throw light on aspects of Hungarian folksong-research which received little or no attention in Bartók's book, conceived as it was as a work of detailed analysis and classification. Reasons of space have prevented the inclusion of many examples, and this is one of the reasons why the reader is often referred to Bartók's work for additional examples. Our knowledge has increased since Bartók's time, particularly with regard to the music of linguistically-related peoples. The relationship of folk music with art-music of all periods and with church music, that is to say, with the historical environment, has become much clearer. The work of collectors —sporadic between 1924 and 1950, but energetically extended with the use of the tape recorder since then—has brought to light many new facts and a considerable number of variants.

Bartók's book retains its value as a reference work and as a well-arranged collection of examples; while the great anthology now in preparation by the Folk Music Research Group, to be published in successive volumes, is designed to complete Bartók's outline. Five volumes of *A Magyar Népzene*

Tára (Corpus Musicae Popularis Hungaricae) have so far appeared, namely: *I Children's Games, II Calendar Customs' Songs, III Wedding Songs, IV Pairing Songs, V Laments*. The Hungarian Academy of Sciences has guaranteed uninterrupted publication of the results of this monumental undertaking. Only when it is completed can a final survey and comparative analysis be carried out. It is also essential that systematically classified collections of the other nations concerned be made available for study.

In the meantime, this book may serve to point the way to greater gains from the comparative study of musical folklore.

Budapest, 1960

Zoltán Kodály

NOTE ON THE NEW ENGLISH EDITION

The new edition of *Folk Music of Hungary* has been expanded by the inclusion of a large number of new musical examples, as well as numerous addenda. The overwhelming majority of these were chosen and drafted by Kodály himself; we not only have his own words about this, but also numerous annotations and supplements to his own copies of the book to guide us. The bulk of my work consisted in supplementing the musical examples and references, in accordance with these annotations.

In a few instances, modifications appeared necessary, even though we could no longer obtain guidance from Kodály: where new facts and results had been brought to light which he did not (or was unable to) consider. This was largely true in the fields of laments and instruments, where two new works—the *Laments* volume in the *Corpus Musicae Popularis Hungaricae V*, and Bálint Sárosi's book on instruments in the *Handbuch der europäischen Volksmusikinstrumente*—have considerably augmented earlier knowledge.

In such cases we have endeavoured to incorporate the new facts and, where possible, to make use of Kodály's formulations from other sources, so as to leave the work, as far as possible, in its original form. We have been particularly careful not to attribute to Kodály statements never made by him.

We hope that in this way the work will not sacrifice present timeliness while preserving that character which has already given it historic value.

Budapest, Autumn 1969

Lajos Vargyas

ABBREVIATIONS USED IN THE MUSICAL EXAMPLES

B. = Béla Bartók, K. = Zoltán Kodály, L. = László Lajtha, S. = Gyula Sebestyé
V. S. = Vilmos Seemayer, V. = Béla Vikár, L. V. = Lajos Vargyas.

Signs used in notation:

    = note of uncertain pitch

    = slight extension of value

    = slight shortening of value

    = slight raising in pitch

    = slight lowering in pitch

    = glissando

    = notes joined in this way are sung to one syllable of the text *(melisma)*

CONTENTS

LIST OF PLATES

I THE FOLK MUSIC TRADITION

ORAL AND WRITTEN TRADITIONS

For centuries, the life of European peoples* has been in continuous transition from an unwritten, agrarian folk-culture towards an urban culture of books and factories.

Generally speaking, the folk art of a people reveals what stage has been reached in this transition; but anomalies may exist. Not every aspect of life transforms itself at the same speed, much as water rises to different heights in communicating tubes, if some of the tubes are corked. Different aspects can still live parallel lives together until such time as home industry is displaced by manufacturing industry. Every so often, the process is halted; in Hungary, for example, the rising cost of living during the First World War brought back home weaving and pottery, both of which had fallen into disuse; post-war poverty brought the bagpipes back into fashion.[1] In intellectual development, too, the old can mix with the new in a multitude of ways, and the spread of book-knowledge does not necessarily preclude the survival of ancient oral tradition. Certain sections of the Hungarian peasantry have been able to read and write for centuries. This means that from the sixteenth century onwards, elements of early written culture have been able to penetrate the original culture preserved in oral tradition.

Musically speaking, however, *all* Hungarians (including the middle classes) were in a state of illiteracy up to the end of the nineteenth century (with the exception of the Middle Ages)[2]: they had no knowledge of written music. Their musical life still showed all the characteristic external signs of traditional oral culture; written music was only used in exceptional instances. Unaccompanied solo songs—the chief, in fact, the only musical activity—were passed from mouth to mouth, and not by writing or notation; old and new alike were disseminated entirely by aural means. Even where written music was seemingly indispensable—as in male-voice choirs—it only served to help

* The Hungarian word *nép*, rendered in German as *Volk*, is constantly adopted by Prof. Kodály when he speaks of 'people' in a national as well as in a folk sense. Unfortunately the English word 'folk' is not so flexible, and a distinction has to be made. (Translator's note.)

memorize the text. Music was learnt entirely by ear. Nor did musical settings in hymnbooks mean much to their users either. Peasants have looked at them since 1607 (when the first Hungarian psalmbook with music was published), and still have not learnt to read them. The tunes have been kept alive by oral tradition, and this is the reason for the existence of many variants.

From the middle of the nineteenth century onwards, in the capital and in various country towns, a handful of the élite, with 'literate' cultural pretensions, gradually developed a musical life comparable with that of West-European cities. But it was a minority compared with the mass of the nation. Even at the end of the nineteenth century, the musical life of the majority lagged behind their general culture, and wore the insignia of the unlettered oral tradition.

When, about 1900, a great surge of interest in folksong and folk music occurred, most Hungarians incorrectly regarded the widely diffused popular music current at the time as the folk-tradition.

POPULAR ART-SONG

In essence, this output of song belongs to the middle of the nineteenth century. The authors had the same attitude and outlook as their public; they represented a transitional type of man: one who had already outgrown folk-culture, but had not yet reached a higher cultural level. Whether young or old, the average Hungarian recognized and loved himself as reflected in their songs.

The authors lacked musical knowledge; in some cases they did not even know enough to write down their own songs correctly, let alone provide them with piano accompaniments. They could only bring their works before the public with help of others. But if *they* could not write, neither could their public read. It was useless for them to publish their songs, since very few people could play or sing from written music. The masses learnt them by ear in the popular theatres, from popular singers or gipsy bands. It was no rare thing for an individual to know several hundred songs, and yet not to know how to read music. They would probably copy the song texts or buy printed collections. These appeared with notation, but no one could read it.

All this is typical of a semi-developed musical life: art-music revealed itself in the forms of oral folk-culture. In many ways it is reminiscent of the fifteenth and sixteenth centuries in France and Germany, when unaccompanied solo melodies flourished in a similar way, and were associated with every aspect of life. To live meant to sing. There, too, it was common for tune and accompaniment to be written by different individuals. But despite the striking resemblance, it is probable that in those centuries more people were able to read song-collections with musical settings than was possible in Hungary; for

14

Western Europe had been living an urban life for centuries. Hungarian town life developed slowly, and only at the end of the nineteenth century did it begin to reach the stage at which musical literacy forms an organic part of community life.

It is for the Hungarian song-historian to study the origin and development of this popular art-song literature. The folklorist is only concerned with that part which was taken over into folk usage, and hence was modified to a greater or lesser degree. These changes have still to be summarized and analysed.[3] Doubtless they will help us to understand popular taste and stylistic tendencies; all the more readily, since we have the original form set down in writing. It is much easier to study the formative function of oral tradition by comparing popular variants of art music, than by analysing the variants of folk music in the stricter sense, where no original form can be demonstrated.

This popular art-music is also ethnographically interesting because a group of songs of the young peasant generation was clearly under its influence. The art-music that came to the village had the effect of stimulating folk-tradition to creative development, thus leading to the appearance of new and previously unknown forms.

THE OLD SONG-TRADITION

Notwithstanding the influence of popular art-song, Hungarian peasants still sing thousands of songs that have nothing in common with nineteenth-century art-music. It is with these that the folklorist is primarily concerned. In them, if anywhere, must be sought the kind of music that, as an organic part of folk-culture, was associated with Hungarian life for hundreds and even thousands of years, the origin of which, like that of the people and the language, is lost in the mists of antiquity.

To get acquainted with this music tradition has been as long and difficult a process as the tracing of the history of folk poetry. As early as 1803, the poet Mihály Csokonai was writing, 'Listen attentively to the singing of the village girl and the simple peasant in the vineyard,' while in 1826 an outstanding man of letters and author of the Hungarian national anthem, Ferenc Kölcsey, observed that 'the seeds of a truly national poetry must be looked for in the songs of the common people'; yet the first folksong collections (including Erdélyi's and Kriza's important publications) still mix the poetry of oral tradition with popular pieces by known writers.[4] Not until the publication of the texts of many Hungarian folksongs, edited by L. Arany and P. Gyulai in 1872, did stricter selection begin.[5] But the texts still await careful analysis and critical stylistic assessment, not to mention comparison with earlier literature and with foreign folk poetry.

Musically speaking, it took even longer for concepts to be clarified. Ádám Pálóczi-Horváth, to whom Hungary owes the most comprehensive of the older song-collections[6] (1814), was no folksong collector in the true sense. He wished only to record tunes he knew. He threw together material of all kinds in a kaleidoscopic mixture: old folk tunes, new art-songs, hymns, tunes composed by himself or others, and so on. Taken as a whole, it is a remarkable document of cultural history. Like the manuscript of István Tóth, cantor of Fülöpszállás (1832–1843), it can have had no influence on the public, since it remained unpublished. Tunes occur in Tóth's manuscript which even today, however, can be described as folksongs.

Franz Liszt might well have become the first Hungarian folksong collector and researcher. In 1838, he writes:[7] 'It was my intention to go into the most backward districts of Hungary... alone, on foot, with a knapsack on my back. But it came to nought.' It is startling to think where we should be today, had he carried out a task that has taken almost a century to complete! But even if his passing fancy had been transformed into reality, it is clear that he could not have been entirely successful. It was immensely difficult for persons from the cultured classes of the nineteenth century to approach the peasants. A typical instance is recorded by the poet Benedek Virág:[8] 'The other day, at sunset,' he wrote to his friend Kazinczy in 1803, 'I was sitting by my window and heard a clear voice singing, "I follow your steps in vain, my sweetheart"; then a sudden outburst of shouting prevented me from hearing more. Perhaps some of you know this song? If so, do let me have it, dear friend, and also any other gay or humorous songs—whatever you have!' It was, in fact, like looking through a window, glimpsing a bird's-eye view of another world. Kazinczy lived seven days' journey away, yet Virág asked him to supply the rest of a song that he could easily have obtained for himself by going outside his own gate. Countless other examples exist, up to our own day. So little were the peasants and their songs known to the nobility and the educated classes who lived in their midst. It was as though an impenetrable barrier lay between them.

Goethe, son of a respectable, urban, bourgeois family, came much closer to the peasants. Not only was he himself a folksong collector, like his friend Herder, whom he greatly admired; in his own poetry, too, he realized what the Hungarian poet Kölcsey had so ardently desired, yet had failed to achieve for all his unceasing, wellnigh superhuman effort—a national poetry, resting on firm folk foundations. (See the latter's: *Nemzeti hagyományok* [National Heritages] 1826.) In Hungary, this became the heritage of the following generation only through an implacably slow historical process, which it would have been difficult to speed up by individual effort. Hence, it is doubtful whether Liszt *could* have reached the peasants, even had he been physically present among them.

Bagpipers from Hont County (Ipolyság, 1911)

Zither player. Cigánd, Zemplén County

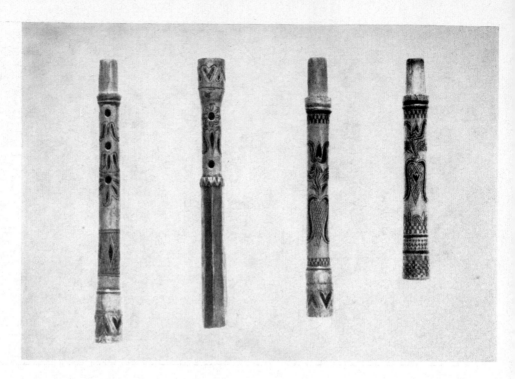

The four component parts of a long shepherd's pipe *(hosszú furulya)*. Somogyudvarhely, Somogy County

Three zithers from the Csongrád County Museum at Szentes, showing the finger board *(kótafa)*, the large head *(nagyfej)*, and three small heads *(kisfej* or *kölyökfej)*

COLLECTIONS WITH TUNES

For the most part, collectors and editors of songs never bothered with the tunes which, as far as their records go, might never have existed. Texts were regarded as literature devoid of melody, even though they had no independent existence amongst the peasants. Any attempt at faithful recording should regard it as axiomatic that tune and text be noted down together. It is, after all, this duality, combining in a higher unity, which constitutes the fundamental nature of 'folksong.' Many Hungarian collectors were aware of this; Dániel Mindszenty and János Udvardy even expressed it in writing. It is most unfortunate that neither their writings nor their collections ever appeared in print. János Erdélyi, editor of the first major collection of Hungarian folksong texts (1846–48), was also aware of the importance of the tunes. Of the collector's task he wrote: '...as far as possible he should devote his care and attention to the *music* of the folksongs to be collected, so that a number of valuable examples of these significant and typical vehicles of Hungarian folk poetry... preserved from oblivion, may come to the knowledge of the cultured public...' (*Népdalok és mondák* Vol. I, p. 7.) It was not his fault that, of the thousand or so sent to him, only twelve appeared in print.[9]

The few publications that have appeared since the mid-nineteenth century almost invariably repeat the same 100 to 200 tunes (Füredi, Mátray, Bognár, Szini), and it was István Bartalus's collection, completed fifty years after Erdélyi's, that had the widest scope to date. It was asking too much, however, to expect him to link tunes with texts that had appeared, in the meantime, without them. Many such texts, generally the most valuable, have never since found their melodies.

At the turn of the century, folksong collecting gathered new impetus, and within a short period unexpected treasures were discovered. The First World War was an insuperable barrier to regular collection, and it also had the effect of jolting peasants out of their old culture and into divergent paths. The first systematic account of these investigations could not appear until 1924. This was Béla Bartók's basic study *A magyar népdal* (Hungarian Folk Music), with 320 tunes. (Published in English in 1931 by the Oxford University Press.) In 1923, 150 Székely songs appeared in Bartók and Kodály's *Erdélyi magyarság, népdalok* (Folksongs of Hungarians of Transylvania). In 1934, the Hungarian Academy of Sciences decided to undertake publication of a complete collection of Hungarian folk tunes. The volumes so far published are:

I *Gyermekjátékok* (Children's Games), 1951.

II *Jeles napok* (Calendar Customs' Songs), 1952.

III *Lakodalom* (Wedding Songs), 1955.

IV *Párosítók* (Pairing Songs), 1959.

V *Siratók* (Laments), 1966.

This publication will be referred to as CMPH *(Corpus Musicae Popularis Hungaricae)* I, II, III, IV and V.

Even this recent and unfinished collection shows that Hungary has been living more deeply steeped in folk-culture than had ever been realized, and that even in the twentieth century much of the original stratum of the Magyar spirit has remained a living reality.

This is evident from the collection of gramophone records, pioneered by the Hungarian Academy of Sciences and continued by the Radio and by the Ethnographical Museum (phonograph records Pátria)—the most significant event of recent years in the sphere of folk music. Up to the outbreak of the Second World War, the collection comprised 107 discs with more than 550 tunes. In 1949, the recordings were continued by the Ministry of People's Culture. The number of discs has now reached 159, and collection continues to the present, the 'Folk Music Research Group' of the Hungarian Academy of Sciences, established in 1953, has collected some 60,000 variants—the greater part of them on wire or tape—which have not yet been worked up. These recordings of songs and games, performed by peasant singers and instrumentalists, reflect folk music with every nuance of the original performance.

A few examples from the deeper strata were certainly included in nineteenth-century collections of folksongs but, understandably, greater numbers could only be brought to light when collectors concerned themselves exclusively with the folk level at which the remains of the old folk-culture still survived: the peasantry at its least civilized level.[10] In 1848, Erdélyi, for example, had brought out a five-line fragment of the ballad 'Kőmíves Kelemen,' of which dozens of versions were discovered even after 1900. In 1848, it was certainly still known and sung in many more places. But the collectors of those days, with perhaps the single exception of János Kriza, were only concerned with songs that had risen to the middle classes, not with songs of the peasantry; they failed to take the decisive 'ten steps' from the manor-house to the peasant's hovel.

It is those 'ten steps' that have been responsible for the results obtained by more modern collectors. Every trace of the ancient stratum of the Magyar spirit had withdrawn into these hovels, while the more civilized part of the nation which had sprung from this culture had sloughed it off, in striving after a newer, higher, and in part foreign, culture. This was doubtless a natural process of development, but the middle class accepted so many foreign immigrants[11] that even today it has not been able to assimilate them completely; in their successors there is usually no trace, either of Hungarian folk-tradition, or of feeling for it. Even aristocrats of ancient Hungarian lineage abandoned it, except for the few who lived in villages alongside the peasants.

Károly Szini's preface to his song-collection (1865) described certain songs as 'folksongs of the nobility'; these were generally in iambic metre and foreign in origin or spirit. He noticed even then that the nobility were much attached to them.[12] Peasants too called them 'noble tunes,' 'noble songs,' just as they did the more sophisticated popular art-songs.

'Peasant song,' on the other hand, was an equivocal term, so long as a pejorative nuance was attached to it over most of the Hungarian-speaking area. In general, 'village song' and 'town song' adequately describe the contrast between folksong and art-song. It would be pointless to attempt a more accurate definition, for owing to the complexity of peasant class-structure, even 'peasant song' is an inadequate description.

THE MEANING OF FOLK-TRADITION

After a century and a half of cultural evolution, it began to be clear that Hungary's anonymous masses represented not only an enormous hidden reserve of material and moral strength, but also a chief storehouse of her cultural riches. It took time for this to be appreciated. János Erdélyi wrote that when a 'national literature has given definite signs of cultural progress it usually turns with great affection to its own folk poetry. Appreciation of the unlettered classes and their poetry seems to require a certain level of development.'

It was far more than a literary and musical phenomenon when the best of the nation turned to the peasantry in an endeavour to understand them and to raise their status; it was a turning-point in a long drawn-out historical process of great importance—a regenerative process, begun when Hungary lay weak and exhausted after the Turkish wars, and still operative today. The unconscious aim was and is the formation of a homogeneous nation in which every member performs his task against the background of a common view of life. The Western nations, now so much more homogeneous than Hungary, have had to fight time and again for this ideal.

Folk poetry and folk music have their part to play in this struggle. Interest in them revives, and they become fused into the life of literature and music, transformed into a fertile creative force that is one of the signs of the nation's will to live, and of the strength that preserves 'cultural identity,' integrating it with its traditional character.[13] János Erdélyi was clear about this: 'We can only make cultural progress through a disciplined fusion of facts and convictions, so that we may become fully aware of our own nationhood and national pride in human terms, and are consciously able to comprehend our historical entity.' The only pity is that we were too quickly satisfied with the result. When Ágoston Greguss made his commemorative address on Erdélyi to the Hungarian Academy, he stated: 'The aim of Erdélyi's life was to make the nation aware of its own soul, and all praise to him, for he succeeded!' But alas! we are still so far from succeeding! Erdélyi merely began the process, for the problem is insoluble and endless. And because we have so often thought the process complete, very few people have persevered, and much valuable time has been wasted.

THE CLASSIFICATION OF FOLK-TRADITION

What is folksong? To this question no one has as yet given a satisfactory answer.[14]

An easier way of approaching this difficult subject is to ask: What do village people sing? Sometimes one or two 'fashionable songs of Budapest' are to be heard even in villages that continue in the old folk-culture. They are sung by isolated individuals who have visited the town, acquired an urban veneer, and are eager to show off. But these songs never gain general currency, and it would be wrong to imagine that the whole village knows nothing else. Their presence gives rise to much premature lamentation of the death of folk-song, though in fact it is still flourishing and enjoyed a period of unparalleled vitality in the ten years before the First World War. The poet Mihály Babits alludes to it in his polemical article on the folksong (*Világ*, 1917). Certain tunes, recorded as rarities about 1910, and then known only to a few old people, were widely known some ten or twenty years later. But in any given year, it is almost impossible to determine the song-repertory of any country, however small. The latest collections—and in particular the recordings of the Hungarian Radio, and especially those of the Folk Music Research Group of the Hungarian Academy of Sciences—show that the older types are still alive and have kept their characteristic mode of performance. Some tunes may have died out, certain districts may have lost their ethnographical importance, while others have only recently been investigated. During the Second World War the Székely population of Bukovina settled in Hungary, choosing Transdanubia as their permanent home. To the same region came many Moldavian Csángó Hungarians also. In consequence, numerous Transylvanian Székely settlers now live in the vicinity of Buda and other areas. Intensive collection of their songs, and research in Rumania, have brought to light new types of tunes and valuable variants of familiar melodies. Again, two archaic regions in Hungary, the vicinity of Somogy County and Szabolcs-Szatmár County, have become a focal point of research-interest through the study of their dances, in respect of dance and other folk music.[15]

Folk-tradition is not to be thought of as one uniform, homogeneous whole. It varies fundamentally according to age, social and material conditions, religion, education, district and sex. Around 1910, a sharp enough difference existed between the song-repertories of the three main ages of life. The middle-aged and elderly people in the village not only did not sing the songs of the young people, but generally did not know them. Still less did the young people know the songs of the older generation, for they were rarely, if ever, sung. Village etiquette only recognized the right of a married man or woman to sing at weddings, in church and on other exceptional occasions, and even then only indoors. Old men or women were considered to be indisputably drunk if they sang outdoors. To sing in the streets or fields was the privilege of the young. The rigour of this unwritten law varied according to the district, but in any case it was always difficult to get the older people to sing.

Any link between the repertory of younger and older people would be known to the grandparents rather than the parents. The reason is to be sought in the nature of village life; grandparents often took care of the children in place of the parents, who went to work all day. In this way, children could hear (from one or other grandparent) songs never to be heard from their parents. The music of children's games spreads under special conditions: it undergoes the least change, if any, since it is handed down by children among themselves.

To a town-dweller of that time, the best-known repertory was that of the middle-aged. They were able to sing everything that came into fashion in the heyday of the romanticizing 'folk plays' (1840–1900). No wonder—for their youth coincided with the period when the whole country echoed with them. Older people knew little of these songs and young people even less. The older generation maintained enough of the old folk-tradition to be able to give us at least some idea of it, and to enable us to discover its strong similarity to songs of ethnic groups related to the Hungarians. They also preserved a few pieces that threw light on the music of sixteenth and seventeenth-century Hungarian lyrics. The younger generation, meantime, assimilated foreign influences and nineteenth-century art-songs, developing new forms in the process, and also becoming much more old-fashioned than their fathers—as if they were reaching out once more towards the traditions of the old generation.

Any classification on the basis of age alone tends to undergo cleavage along the lines of two further categories, however, the social and the regional. Village society is a unity only when viewed from a distance. The more closely it is studied, the more gradations of difference appear. A major difference is occupation (artisans and agricultural workers, farm servants, shepherds). Within these categories differences arise from property-ownership and religion. This is also reflected in the songs that are known: the well-to-do like to distinguish themselves from the poorer even in their songs. 'We knew that one, but didn't think much of it,' said a farmer (from Farkasd in Nyitra County in 1905) of the ballad 'Sági bíróné'; he had twenty acres of land which he worked himself. Prosperous farmers of the Alföld (Hungarian Plain) looked askance at the *gányó* (tobacco-farmer) song. The more closely the farmer approaches the status of the small-holding nobility in property and way of life, the less interesting does he become to the ethnographer. Once above a certain property-level, it is no longer correct for the farmer's daughter to sing, and even less for the farmer. The artisan class is one degree more urban. Generally they are good singers, but rarely do they offer any interesting material to the ethnographer. At times a certain musical ambition shows itself even in the lower levels of society. A coachman's wife from Szatmár County said to us: 'I have always preferred these "noble" songs.'

Regional differences cut decisively across the classifications according to age and occupation. In the more 'civilized' districts, the repertory of even the poorest has come under town influence. It is in more old-fashioned districts with the same social conditions and age groups, that the most valuable material is to be found. Even today for instance in Moldavia (Rumania), young Hungarian girls can be heard singing in chorus in the old-fashioned, ornate style, such as could only be heard from the oldest villagers in 1910, and even then only individually.

The oldest and most beautiful Székely melodies were heard in Csík County (Transylvania) from even well-to-do farmers, while in the more civilized counties of Udvarhely and Marosszék these same tunes have come to be known as 'beggars' songs,' that is, they have 'sunk' to the lowest level of society. Ballads are still known to everyone in Csík, Moldavia and Bukovina. In Marosszék, they are often sung by the gipsies, as are Christmas carols in most parts of the country. Fragments of ancient Hungarian hymns are also preserved among gipsy beggars by a similar process.

Last of all comes classification by sex. Certain songs are only to be heard from women, others only from men. Generally speaking, women have a richer repertory; usually they know men's songs as well, though they never sing them for their own pleasure. Of the 150 Székely (Transylvanian) folksongs in the Bartók–Kodály: *Folksongs of Hungarians of Transylvania*, only thirty-two are sung by men, twenty-three are uncertain, so that at least two-thirds are women's songs. In Transylvania, moreover, old men sing more readily than anywhere else, and know more songs. Songs for mourning (that is, laments), for betrothals and weddings, and to a great extent ballads, too, are sung exclusively by women. The feminine spirit tends to be the guardian of folk religion and superstition, and it is also the storehouse of music and poetry.

II THE PRIMITIVE STRATUM OF HUNGARIAN FOLK MUSIC

The social function of folksong can only be fully understood in relation to the various classifications outlined in the previous chapter. The importance of individual songs and song types has to be examined in relation to the everyday life of the people. In other words, it is as important to know the purpose served by the songs as to know the songs themselves. There is a pressing need for further research aimed at filling this gap in our knowledge.

But even when songs are classified by social background and purpose, it is clear that they still do not constitute stylistic types. The discrimination of these requires meticulous examination of the entire material, bewildering in its variety. Even after popular art-songs have been eliminated, not one style, but a whole series of styles unfolds. Which of these is the root-style of Hungarian musical idiom, and which are offshoots, imported styles and grafted borrowings? Even today, none of these questions can be satisfactorily answered, partly for lack of study, and partly for lack of necessary material. Some of it will never be available.

Linguistics and archaeology have already shed considerable light on the origin of the Hungarians. They can be traced back to their beginnings; but neither they nor any of the peoples with whom they came into contact from the fifth to the fifteenth century have left us a single contemporary musical document. The development of Hungarian music, however, cannot have been different from that of the language or of the people. Wherever the people went, and at whatever pace they developed, music went with them. Whatever influenced the language was capable of influencing the music as well. Since there is no hope of obtaining contemporary data, it is to the music of related and neighbouring peoples, or of their successors, that we must turn in order to study related characteristics. Unfortunately, this music still awaits investigation, for the scientific approach to it has only just begun. The Finns are the only related people to have made rich musical collections. Their music is so distant and fundamentally so different from that of the Hungarians, however, that up to now no significant connections have been established between them.[16]

CONNECTIONS WITH RELATED PEOPLES

In the Volga region live a small people related to the Hungarians, the Mari or Cheremis. What has so far been discovered of their music has shown such surprising and basic similarity to one stratum of Hungarian folk music that an ancient relationship between the two peoples can hardly be doubted. It is the more obvious, in that this very stratum in the Hungarian song-repertory is that which stands out as foreign in Europe and yet can be shown to exist wherever Hungarians are living. Even when its archaic types have died out, or survive only among the old people, they have been preserved in a different form among the young people as an organic continuation of the old.

It is a stratum characterized by the pentatonic scale and by repetition of the first phrase at the fifth below. The following is a tune well known all over Hungary. Even amongst the cultured classes, nearly every Hungarian knows it, or some variant of it. The folk play *A falu rossza* (The Village Villain) is largely responsible for its popularity. (See Coll. Bartalus: I, 48; many variants CMPH, Vol. III.)

Bartók, No. 243.

The second half is an exact repetition of the first, at the fifth below. This fifth construction is a constant feature of Mari music. The pentatonic scale is predominant, to the exclusion of other scales, and in a form without semitones which appears to be native to Turco-Tartar peoples living on the steppes of Central Asia as far East as China:

In the tune just quoted, a_2, e_2 and a_1 also occur in addition to these five notes. In the second half of Mari tunes, however, that is, in the repetition of the first half, a new pentatonic construction is often introduced. If the tune is analysed in this way the first half is seen to be built on one pentatonic scheme *dfgac* and the second on another: *gbbcdf*, with only a single unemphasized passing note, extraneous to the pentatonic set. In the first half, the extraneous

24

note is e_2, in the second it is a_1. Such extraneous notes occur even where pentatonic systems are in full bloom. Chinese theory knows them by the name of *pien*.

In Hungarian music, where almost every European scale is in use alongside the pentatonic, the surprising thing is not that pentatonic systems are so often admixed with extraneous notes under the influence of heptatonic scales, but that they have remained so uncontaminated.

A variant of this tune is to be found in Bartók, No. 244. It is known only in the Southern Transdanubian villages; numerous variants have come to light from newer collections:

3

Note by note, the second half imitates the first exactly at the fifth below. Both halves belong to the same pentatonic scheme, and only in the ornamentation is there an extraneous note. The tune is pentatonic, but its third and seventh are a semitone higher than usual. Instead of $gb\flat cdf$ it has $gbcdf\sharp$, a peculiarity of Transdanubian tunes. The intonation of these notes is not always clear. Sometimes they are sung lower, sometimes higher, intonation varying even with the same singer. Again, in certain Transdanubian tunes, there are only minor thirds and minor sevenths. This tune also has minor variants:

AP 4483/g. Karácodfa (Baranya County), 1962. L.V.

4

It is worthy of note that the lower f persists when there is $f\sharp$ above. A peculiar development of the feeling of tonality[17] affected the pitch of individual notes, but could not change the construction and pattern of the melody. Being rootedly pentatonic, the tunes are not subject to the characteristic melodic pattern of major tonality.

25

Compare the following Mari tune[18]:

oį ä-t'ä-żən d-t'ä żə maż əm Ba-ra maɼ-ə-ret? etc.

These two tune-lines are inconsistently quoted in Lach's notes as I-I-II or I^2-I-II or I^2-I. One glance at the Mari collections makes clear that this is only half a tune. It is complete only if the section quoted is repeated a fifth lower:

The notes marked with an asterisk are not fifths of their corresponding notes in the first half, because the fifth $e\flat$ does not exist in the g-$b\flat$ cd-f pentatonic scheme. In such cases, the second half of Mari songs has the lower (and less frequently the upper) adjacent note instead of the fifth.[19]

In tunes that belong to a single five-note scheme, the precision of the fifth construction is sacrificed in order to preserve the pentatonic system. Originally, the two did not go together. Note for note correspondence is only possible within the same scheme when the tonic, the Chinese *kung* (in our notation $b\flat$), does not occur in the first part.

It is not, however, the presence of the *kung* that decides whether the tune is built up on a single, or tonal, scheme or on a double, or real, scheme (with a new *do*, a fifth lower, in the second part). The following (Ex. No. 7a) is a tune from Surd (Somogy County, V. S.), and underneath (Ex. No. 7b) is given a Mari parallel from Eshpaj (*Piesni naroda mari*, Moscow, 1930, No. 4).

The first note of the second part of the tune is not a fifth but a fourth lower, although the scheme contains the fifth. Why? Because the mutual attraction of keynote and fifth is so strong that it asserts itself even when the scheme would permit an exact transposition at the fifth below. The same thing happens when the fifth in the answer *(comes)* of a tonal fugue corresponds to the keynote of the subject *(dux)* and vice versa. This example is of particular importance because in the latter half of the second part it begins at the regular distance of a fifth, while at the beginning of the second half tonal attraction has prevailed. The form is in fact A^5A^5AA, that is, it has been developed from a single melodic cell. It is all the more significant that the Mari variant also follows this tonal-real variation. The leap of a fourth at the beginning of the tune is answered at the beginning of the second half by the leap of a fifth. This means that all the other notes of the third line are a whole tone higher in the pentatonic scheme until the fourth line reasserts the regular distance at the fifth.

The similarity between the tunes is even more evident if the first note of each line of the Mari tune is left out. The Mari version is simpler and more archaic, the Hungarian more developed—the endings of the first and second lines do not follow the pattern. At the end of the second line, the pattern calls for *d* (see Exs. Nos. 12–26), but *d* is commonly replaced by *bb* (Ex. No. 7) or even by *g* (Exs. Nos. 8–10), and indeed by *c* (Ex. No. 11) in variants of Hungarian pentatonic tunes.

Kákics (Baranya County), 1930. L.

Menyhe (Nyitra County). K.

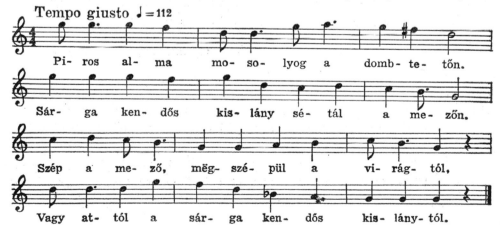

10

The following example shows how tonal attraction makes itself felt at the beginning as well as at the end of the tune-lines. The last note of the third line answers the *g* of the first with *d*. Frequently the distance of the fourth which occurs at this point is maintained to the end of the tune.

Borsosberény (Nógrád County). L.

11

Szentgyörgyvölgye (Zala County). V.

12

Gyimesközéplok (Csík County), 1912. L.

13

Although it is clear that in its amended form the Mari tune (Exs. Nos. 5–6) is musically the same as the Hungarian one quoted as Exs. No. 3 (Bartók: No. 244) and No. 4[20], their formal differences are important. The Hungarian has 2×6 bars, the Mari 2×8. It is exactly the same as the Hungarian with the omission of the two pairs of bars in brackets. This form sometimes occurs in Mari tunes (see for example a variant of this tune in Lach: No. 219). The Hungarian verse-form is reminiscent of the rhyme scheme *aabaab*, and the *tripertitus caudatus* of the Middle Ages, and may be attributed to Western European influence. Medieval hymn-poetry may well have transmitted similar forms to Hungary before they became common knowledge through the 'Simeon éneke' (Song of Simeon) of French origin, and the six-line 'Balassa verse' (number of syllables $= 2 \times 6.6.7$) which too was assimilated into the folk repertory.

It is possible, however, that the Western *aabaab* form found a corresponding original form in Hungary, springing from an Eastern source. This seems to be corroborated by the fact that a few Mari and Chuvash songs of similar structure are known. The Mari song under discussion has another Hungarian counterpart with 2×8 bars, the Transdanubian 'Swineherd's Song':

Karád (Somogy County), 1934. K.

The great antiquity of this tune type (with line-endings $\boxed{7}$ $\boxed{5}$ $\boxed{\flat 3}$) is shown by its widespread popularity and by the existence of countless variants with different syllable-counts. Apart from 6- and 13–14-syllable forms (see No. 7 and the 'Swineherd's Song' quoted above [No. 14]) variants exist with from 7 to 12 syllables. Compare the following examples (Nos. 15 to 23) and the tune from Farkasd (Nyitra County; No. 24):

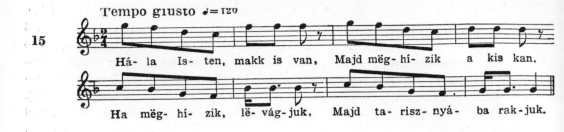

15

Tempo giusto ♩=120

Há- la Is- ten, makk is van, Majd mëg- hí- zik a kis kan.

Ha mëg- hí- zik, lë- vág- juk, Majd ta- risz- nyá- ba rak- juk.

Mezőkövesd (Borsod County), 1929. V. S.

16

Tempo giusto

Sej, roz- ma- ring, roz- ma- ring, Lë- sza- kadt ró- lam az ing,

Van már né- këm Kö- ves- dën, Ki mëg- varr- ja jaz in- gëm.

a) Romhány (Nógrád County), b) Csíkmadaras (Csík County), c) Fedorov 104.

17 a

Nin-csen a- pám, nin-csen a- nyám, Az Is- ten is ha- rag- szik- rám.

b

Ú- ton me-gyen a ka- to- na, Ud- va- ron áll Mó-nár An- na.

c ♪=148

Ár- va vagyok mint a gó- lya, Ki- nek nin-csen párt-fo- gó- ja.

Haj, azt mond-ja a ka- to- na, Je- re ve-lem Mó-nár An- na.

Tempo giusto ♩=120

Volt ne-këm ëgy kecs-kém, tu-dod–ë? Kert-be rë- kesz-tët-tem, tu-dod–ë?

Mëg- öt- te a far-kas, tu-dod–ë? Csak a szar-vát hagy-ta, lá- tod-ë?

Istensegíts (Bukovina). 1914. K.

Tempo giusto ♩=88,96

Tú- rót ë- szik a ci-gány, du-ba; Ve- sze- kë-dik az-u-tán, lë-ba.

Még azt mond-ja: po-fon-vág, du-ba; Vág- ja biz a nagy-ap-ját, lë-ba.

Perőcsény (Hont County), 1912. K.

In dance-step

Tul-só so- ron nyi-lik a vi- rág, E-gész éj- jel ér-zem a sza- gát;

Ki- re ves-sem fe- ke- te sze- mem, Ki vi-gasz-tal- ja meg a szi- vem?

Gyergyószentmiklós (Csík County), 1910. K.

Allegretto

Bár csak en-gëm va-la-ki, va-la- ki, Hor-dó fúr-ni hí-na ki, hí-na ki!

Ki- fúr-nám a hor-dó-ját, hor-dó-ját, Mëg-in-nám a jó bo-rát, jo bo-rát!

22

Tempo giusto ♩=70

Bé- res le- gény, jól meg- rakd a sze- ke- ret,

Sar- ju- tüs- ke bö- kö- di a te- nye- red!

Men- nél job- ban bö- kö- di a te- nye- red,

An- nál job- ban rakd mĕg a sze- ke- re- det.

Nagybajom (Somogy County). K.

23

Hol jár- tál az éj- jel ci- nĕ- ge ma- dár?

Ab- la- kod- ba vol- tam, drá- ga vi- o- lám.

Mért nem ko- pog- tat- tál ci- nĕ- ge ma- dár?

Fél- tem az u- rad- tól, drá- ga vi- o- lám.

The following type is widely spread both in Hungary and the East.[21] We quote a Hungarian tune recorded by the author at Farkasd (Nyitra County) in 1905 (the nineteenth-century text adopted by a wide cross-section of the peasantry is by G. Czuczor), with a Mari tune below (Ex. No. 24; Vasiliev, 1923, No. 96) and a Chuvash variant (Ex. No. 25; Maximov, 1932, No. 87).

24

Poco parlando

Ka- la- pom a Ti- szán usz- kál, Su- bám zá- log a bi- ró- nál.

Pu- ro ta- ɲet βok-te- net-ɣân šü- met- kâ- let möl- dâl- deš;

Bagpipe from Somogy
County

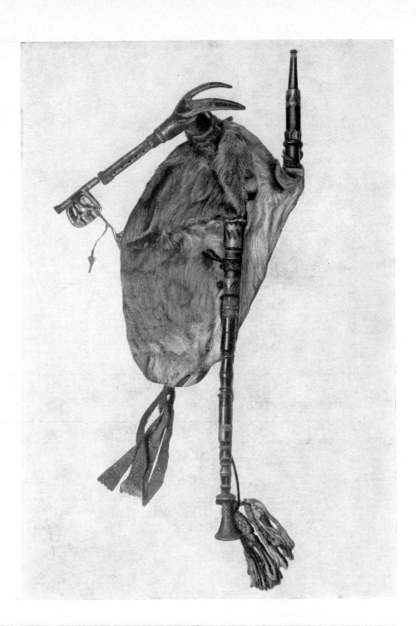

Horse-headed zither
(tambura). Debrecen,
Déri Museum

Making a long shepherd's pipe *(hosszú furulya)* from elderwood. Somogyudvarhely, Somogy County

All three tunes contain two schemes, the first being *d-fga-c*, the second *g-bᵇcd-f*. In the Hungarian tune, the notes marked with an asterisk are unstressed, extraneous passing-notes. The first part of the Hungarian differs slightly from the second, but both parts of the Mari and the Chuvash tunes have the same form. As this complete identity exists in many Hungarian songs, too, we feel justified in assuming that it formerly existed in all Hungarian songs of this type.

Ex. No. 26 is another Hungarian-Mari-Chuvash parallel (*Transylvanian Folksongs:* No. 135; var. in Bartók: a) No. 65; b) Vasiliev, 1923, No. 150; c) Maximov, 1932, No. 88).

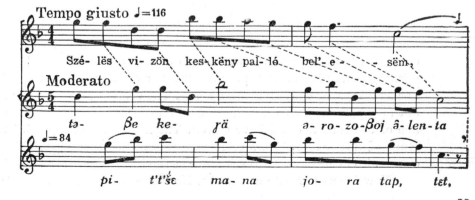

Disregarding the rhythm, the melodic content is seen to be essentially identical, line for line. The eleven-syllable (4+7) construction of the Mari increases in the third and fourth lines to fourteen (8+6 and 7+7). A frequent phenomenon in Mari songs is the inconstancy of the number of syllables to the line as compared with Hungarian songs. The Chuvash text has eight syllables, but may perhaps have altered, since according to the number of notes in each line of the tune it could have eleven. The first notes of the third line of the Hungarian tune do not show correspondence at the fifth below. This sometimes occurs also in Mari and Chuvash songs at the beginning of the third line.

Now let us compare a) Bartók, No. 58 with b) Lach: Cheremis No. 230:

In these eleven-syllabled lines there is no difference in rhythm. At the end of the second line of the Hungarian song, b^b (the third) has replaced the original fifth d. Strictly speaking, at the end of the Mari song it is only permissible to have g_1, the lower fifth of the end of the second line (or f_1 at the end of the second line). Lach's notation must be regarded as corrupt or as evidence of a faulty rendering. The fifth construction is generally so pure in Mari songs that divergencies do not occur. The Mari pentatonic system uses scarcely any extraneous notes; it is as if notes outside the scheme did not exist. Even the ornamentation is formed from notes of the pentatonic system.

Straightforward comparison of Hungarian 'pure examples'[22] with Mari examples are so convincing that fuller comment is unnecessary. But traces of this construction exist in many Hungarian songs that at first sight exhibit a completely different form and style (Exs. Nos. 28, 29).

28

Parlando ♩ = 75

Nem lop-tam én é-le-tem-be. Csak hat ti-nót Deb-re-cen-be:

Ha- za- haj-tot- tam a ti- nót. Mind a hat da- ru- sző- rű volt.

29

Rubato ♩ = cca 72

Ti-szán in-nen, Du-nán túl, Túl a Ti-szán van egy csi-kós nyá-jas- tul.

Kis pej- lo-va ki van köt-vel, Szűr-kö-tél-lel pak-róc nél-kül, gaz-dás- tul.

In the second half of Ex. No. 29, the 3rd, 5th, 6th and 8th notes are in the relation of a fifth, and the 4th and 7th notes of a fourth, to the corresponding notes of the first line. The last three notes of the cadence are a perfect answer at the fifth. In bars three and four of the second half—repetitions of the previous bar—there is naturally no fifth relationship.

The fifth construction may previously have existed here, too; as the controlling formal principle grew weaker in the singer's consciousness, the performers gradually gave up the tradition of exact correspondence at the fifth, so that finally it only appears in cadential notes. This may have happened under the influence of other patterns, or merely from the urge for variation. The remaining traces usually testify to the presence of a five-note skeleton, even where the whole tune is no longer pentatonic.

The construction also appears in all its purity—yet another proof of the extraordinary power of the principle—in various types of heptatonic tunes (Exs. Nos. 30, 31).

30

Parlando

Ma van hus-vét nap- ja, má-sod- éc- ca- ká- ja, Jól tud- já- tok,

Ki- nek el- ső nap-ján Jé- zus fel- tá- mad- ván Di- cső-ség- be.

31

— Hogy-ha el-mész ka-to-ná- nak, Moñ mëg fi- am, hol kap-lak mëg?

— Je- resz ki Ga- li- ci- á- ba S ott mëg-kapsz ëgy kor- cso-má- ba.

A well-known example is the so-called 'Transylvanian Pillow Dance'.

CMPH I, p. 853. Ehed (Maros-Torda County), 1914. B.

32

Döm-bör vaj-da, döm-bör vaj-da, prü-csök-fü- lü kecs - ke.

A- pád is volt vaj- da mes-ter, Li- pic Ke- le - men - ke.

A hi- jú- ba hat to - jás, hogy le - he- tett ben - ne?

Csi-nál-junk egy ron-gyos le - vet, nin-csen e - cet ben - ne.

Pátria record 102/B. Bözöd (Udvarhely County).

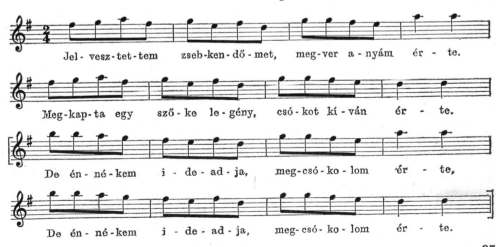

33

Jel- vesz-tet-tem zseb-ken- dő - met, meg-ver a - nyám ér - te.

Meg-kap-ta egy sző- ke le - gény, csó- kot kí - ván ér - te.

De én - né-kem i - de- ad - ja, meg-csó- ko - lom 'ér - te,

De én - né-kem i - de - ad - ja, meg-csó- ko - lom ér - te.

37

Jaj jaj jaj jaj   jaj jaj jaj jaj   (etc. to the end)

The parts included in parentheses are optional repetitions; this is the reason why the text does not extend to the end of the song. These tune types, with their counterparts in Czech, Slovak and Polish folk music, link the Western tonal system with the fifth construction of Eastern origin.

Nothing comparable exists in Mari music, where present data reveal no tonal system other than the pentatonic. In other respects, Hungarian tunes cannot be expected to match any given group of Mari and Chuvash tunes exhibiting pure fifth construction: their musical content has an independent folk character quite different from the Hungarian. To discover the original common heritage of the two peoples, similarity both of construction and musical content needs to be studied. Identical rhythm is particularly striking, even to the unpractised ear, but the comparison shows that even two tunes with different rhythms can basically be the same.

The fifth construction can be represented diagrammatically as follows:

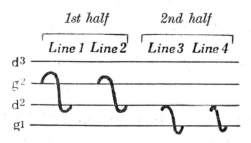

Expressed in letters, the formula is A^5A^5AA. If the second melodic line differs widely from the first, we call it B and obtain the formula A^5B^5AB. But even then, the essentials are two high lines, usually in the range c_2-d_2-bb_2-(d_3) and the same two lines a fifth lower in the range f_1-g_1-d_2-(g_2).

Mari songs also show a related type. The range is small, usually only one octave. (In the previous examples, the range is sometimes as much as two octaves.) The length is not more than eight bars (the previous examples often reach twice that length). The tempo is lively, the performance is metrical and dance-like. Among the first type there are many songs in slow rhythms, with great lyrical sweeps; whilst the second type consists of small motifs of limited range.

The melodic lines could be represented diagrammatically as follows:

35

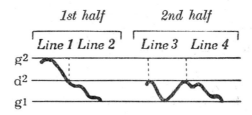

Here the structural basis is obviously related to that of the more extended type. It starts off high, but at the end of the second line it drops to the final. The third line tends to carry out the principle of correspondence at the fifth: the notes of the first line are usually heard a fifth (sometimes a fourth) below (see Note No. 19). But the fourth line does not continue this: it repeats the second line not at the lower fifth, but at the original pitch, with little or no variation. It is characteristic that the tune touches the final note three times. (In exceptional cases, four times, see Lach, Nos. 1–10, 624a and 627a Phonograms of the Hungarian Ethnographical Museum, to be referred to as Ph. E. M.) Its structure is A⁵BAB. This type is also represented in Hungarian folksong: see Ex. No. 36a together with its Mari counterpart, Ex. No. 36b.

a) Ph. E. M. No. 1022b, Karcfalva (Csík County), 1907. B.

b) Ph. E. M. No. 628a.

36 a
b

The only rhythmical difference between the two is that the Hungarian has six syllables in the second line and six in the fourth. This is exceptional; in the rhythm of other similarly constructed Hungarian songs, formal identity with Mari rhythm is complete: 4×7 or 8, 7, 8, 7 or even 4×8 syllables (Exs. Nos. 37, 38).

Bartók, No. 47. Ph. E. M. 15b. Szegvár (Csongrád County). V.

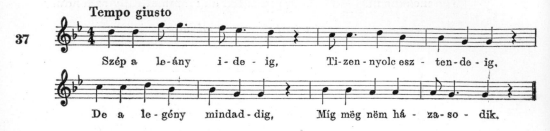

37

Szép a le-ány i-de-ig, Ti-zen-nyolc esz - ten-de-ig,

De a le-gény mindad-dig, Míg mëg nëm há - za-so - dik.

Bartók, No. 10. Ph. E. M. 1635a. Rafajnaújfalu (Bereg County), 1412. B.

38

Minden ember szerencsésen, Csak én é-lek ke - ser - ve-sen;

Fejem le-haj - tom csen-de-sen, Csak ugysi-rok ke-ser - ve-sen.

The variable line-length of some Mari texts has already been mentioned (see p. 34). Under the influence of the $\boxed{\flat 3}$ prevailing in Transylvania, the final of the second line in the Hungarian example (No. 36) jumps to $\boxed{\flat 3}$, that is, bb, instead of $\boxed{1}$, i.e. g—although one variant has a line-ending in g.

At the beginning of the second line (Ex. No. 36), the Hungarian tune drops a note lower, except for the finals of the second and fourth lines. If single sections are compared, the melodic conception is found to be identical with that of the Mari, as if they were note for note the same. The 3-note group bb-a-f corresponds to the group c-bb-g in the second and fourth lines of the Mari tune. Thus an extraneous note, a, appears in the tune. The third line is also one note lower in the Hungarian, not so much as a result of mechanical precision, but rather of pentatonic feeling: here the equivalent of d_2-c_2-bb_1-g_1 is not c_2-bb_1-a_1-f_1, but c_2-bb_1-g_1-f_1. It is possible that originally this occurred at corresponding places in the second and fourth lines, and that only later g came to be replaced by a. It is certainly inconsistent, but does not alter the validity of the two forms. This phenomenon is not surprising in a musical idiom where the pentatonic system is in decay. It may be added that the example comes from a younger singer. For further examples:

40

É- dës a-nyám lá-nya vó-tam Míg sze-re-'tőt něm tar-tot-tam,

Mi- hánt sze-re- tőm a- ka-dott, É- dës a-nyám měg-ta- ga-dott.

Ipolyság (Hont County), 1910. B.

Tempo giusto ♩=148

Ar- ra gye- re a- mő- re én, Maj měg-tu-dod, hol la- kok én:

Csip- ke- bo-kor- ró- zsa mel-lett,—Gye-re ba-bám, měg- ö- lel- lek.

Despite differences in the third line, this type of tune may be recognized in the following (Ex. No. 41):

a) A widespread Transdanubian tune. (Variations: G. Kiss, Ormánság, No. 60, Berze Nagy, *Baranyai néphagyományok* [Folk-Traditions of Baranya]: I, pp. 517 and 567.)

b) A Transylvanian variation.

c) A Mari tune (Lobachev: *12 Detskih piesen*, Moscow, 1930, No. 8).

a) Beleg (Somogy County), 1922. K., b) Ph. E. M. No. 361c. Lengyelfalva (Udvarhely County). V., c) Lobachev, No. 8.

41 a

Lë- e-sëtt a makk a fá- rú, Mozs'gyüttem én a ta-nyá-rú.

Tempo giusto

b

Në huz- zon úgy é- dös ma-mám, Több fi-gyel-mük nincs-csen re-ám?

c

In-gëm, ga-tyám de szeny-nyes, Ma-gam va-gyok sze-rel-mes.

Te-li szëd-tem a kor-só-mat, Meg-öl-tek a nagy gyil-ko-sok.

Let us now compare a Hungarian bagpipe tune (Ex. No. 42a) with a Mari tune (Ex. No. 42b. Variation: Lach, Nos. 109–111, 113, 159a).

a) Mohi (Bars County), 1912. K.
b) Ph. E. M. No. 628b.

42 a

Macs-ka mënt disz-nó-tor-ba, U-tá-na mënt a ku-tya.

b

Ō-mɯž ɼr-na kü-βa-re-šél r̃ ši-l'â kr̃n-at ti jr̃-rá

Ku-tya u-tán a' ffar-kas, Far-kas u-tán a' kka-kas.

Ti kül'-müž laɪ me-l'àn oé šét r̃ ši-l'â kr̃n-at o-nà-tü.

Here some sections of the tune are more disparate, but the melodic line and construction are the same. In the Hungarian example, the pentatonic scheme has yielded to the heptatonic major scale, although it must be remembered that the Mari tune also has major characteristics.[23]

Anticipation of the major triad is clearly demonstrated in one group of Mari tunes, though it does not involve major tonality or the major scale. This last certainly came to Hungary through Western music. In the Hungarian variant, the dominant-tonic relationship is conspicuous; in the Mari tune there is no trace of it. It is possible then that some Hungarian tunes that at first sight appear to be based on a major scheme are similarly rooted in the pentatonic system (see pp. 48–49).

Examples of this construction with a range of less than an octave are also to be found. (Ex. No. 43 with a Mari counterpart.)

a) Bodok (Nyitra County), 1906. K.
b) Ph. E. M. No. 627b.

This is a shrunken version of the previous example. The third and fourth lines only reach the third by interchanging third and fourth. There is still the characteristic leap to the third at the end of the third line. In the Hungarian variant, the relationship of the third line to the first—whether at the fifth or at the fourth—has become indistinct, while in the Mari it is retained with a tonal interchange of fourths and thirds. In some Mari examples (their authenticity is questionable), it has completely disappeared, however, and the second, third, and fourth lines are exactly, or almost, identical: ABBB. (Lach, Nos. 1–11, 13–14, 17–18, 24–25, etc. Also *ibid.*, the above-mentioned Nos. 111 and 113.) Somewhat less closely related, but still in some degree related is the following (Ex. No. 44):

Kászonújfalu (Csík County), 1912. K.

Other Mari and Chuvash tune-types have Hungarian counterparts, as well as those with fifth constructions. Here is an example of the old Hungarian ABBC type (Ex. No. 45a. Var. Bartók, No. 14), and a Mari parallel (Ex. No. 45b. Var. Vasiliev, 1923, No. 43).

a) *Transylvanian Folksongs:* No. 61, b) Vasiliev, 1923, No. 37.

Gyergyóújfalu (Csík County), 1907. B

The content of the second and third tune-lines is slightly different in the Hungarian examples (see also Ex. No. 46), but completely identical in the Mari (as it is also in other Hungarian examples). The Mari fourth line corresponds to the first line at the lower fifth, A⁵BBA. The unexpected closing note reminds us that, in areas where the pentatonic system flourishes, the final is variable. Almost every Hungarian pentatonic tune ends on g_1 *(la₁)*, but among Eastern peoples, tunes are found ending on f_1 (=VII, *so₁*), *b* flat (=♭₃, *do*), c_2 (=4, *re*), and more rarely *d* (=5, *mi*). At some time, this may have been possible in Hungarian tunes, too, as is shown even today in sporadic examples. Compare the following three variants (Exs. Nos. 47, 48, 49):

47

Ár- va va-gyok, nincs gyá-mo-lom,   Még a vi- zet ës gyá-szo-lom.

Ár- va va-gyok mind a ma-dár.   Ki a fel-hőn o- da-fënn jár.

48

Hej, Már két he-te vagy már há-rom, Hogy a szá- ma-dó-mat vá-rom.

A- mo- da gyün, a- mint lá-tom, Fecs- ke- ha-sú sza-már há- ton.

49

Csü - tör-tö-kön virra- dó - ra

Tá - ma-dó áll az aj - tóm - ba.

Hozzák a bé - legző vasat, Hej!

Sze - gény szivem majd meg ha - sad. Hej!

1)   2)   3)   4)   5)

The first has the normal la_1-ending, the second the so_1-ending and the third even has the *do*-ending, although all three basically identical, i. e., they are variants. The following tune (Ex. No. 50a) with a Chuvash parallel also gives a form with a so_1-ending, for which no la_1-variant is as yet known.

a) *Transylvanian Folksongs:* No. 123, b) Maximov, No. 64.

50 a E- zër-nyolc-száz-nëgy-ven-hat-ba El__ këll mën-ni há- bo- rú- ba,

b Ha ugy va-gyon cé-du- láz- va, Hogy el- ve-szëk a csa-tá- ba.

It is possible that many Hungarian folk tunes which today end on g_1 at one time ended on f_1. This is more usual in the East, as the examples below will show.

Tune No. 51 has been preserved by the Székely, who migrated to Bukovina in the eighteenth century, and returned to Hungary in recent years. It is sung in strict $^6/_8$ time. The Mari parallel was published by Vasiliev. It is twice as long, the whole being repeated a fifth lower; so in Hungary, the original fifth construction has been worn down' to half its size. (But there is also a similar Chuvash variant: Fedorov: *146 Chuvash Songs*, Moscow, 1954, No. 140.)

a) *Transylvanian Folksongs:* No. 104. Istensegíts (Bukovina), 1914. K., b) Ph. E. M. No. 3235b. Andrásfalva (Bukovina), 1934., c) Vasiliev, 1934, No. 37.

51 a Ke-rek úc- ca szë- ge- let, Jár-tam én ott e- le- get.

b Ti- zën- há- rom mëg ëgy fél, Ké- ret- te- lek, nem jöt- tél.

c

Ha még ëgy-szër ott já- rok, A ró- zsám-ra ta-lá- lok.
Ha nem jöt- tél hon ül- ə- tél, Lë- já- nyok any-ja lët- tél.

Here, too, at the end, f_1 corresponds to g_1, but in the middle we have f_1 instead of b^b_1. In other tunes, as well as in the Hungarian variants, the second line may end with b^b_1 or f_1. Sometimes both notes occur in the same variant, so that the b^b_1 descends to f_1. A similar interchange is to be noticed at the end of many Hungarian songs: the same tune appears with two different finals. In terms of Western musical theory one variant ends on the tonic *(do)*, the other on the dominant *(so$_1$)* (Exs. Nos. 52, 53).

Bartók, 93c. Vacsárcsi (Csík County), 1907. B.

52 Tempo giusto $\mathbf{J} = 76$

A vacsárcsi halastó, halas - tó, Be-le-jestëm lovastó, lovas - tó.

Jaj Istenëm! Ki vësz ki, hej de ki vësz ki? Sajnál-e még éngëmët va-la - ki?

Bartók, 93b. Horgos (Csongrád County), 1906. B.

53 Tempo giusto

Jaj de sokat a-rat-tam a nyá - ron, De keveset aludtam az á gyon!

Vesd meg rózsám, vesd meg a slingölt ágyadat, Had pihenjem ki magam az a latt!

In most cases the *do*-ending must be regarded as a recent development. In comparing the following pair of tunes, we find that, placed alongside the tonic ending of the Hungarian tune Ex. No. 54a, the dominant ending of its Chuvash equivalent No. 54b makes the form archaic, particularly when it is realized that such endings are in an overwhelming majority in the Chuvash material.

a) Ph. E. M. No. 10b. Csincse (Borsod County). V.

b) Maximov, No. 61.

Without the Chuvash parallel, no one would ever have suspected the existence of the pentatonic scale in the Hungarian tune, the less so since a majority of its variants show flawless major scales; in the variant given here there is no seventh degree. The example should serve to show that seemingly heptatonic tunes may conceal a pentatonic structure, even when no clear pentatonic variant is known, as in the examples below (Ex. No. 55). A third variant, in which *fa* frequently appears, is used in *Háry János* 'Nagyabonyban csak két torony látszik' (Only two towers are to be seen in Nagyabony). Compare the Chuvash tune given on p. 68 (Ex. No. 88).

a) Ph. E. M. No. 415d. Szentábrahám (Udvarhely County). V.

b) Hódmezővásárhely (Csongrád County). Péczely.

Goatherd playing the short shepherd's pipe *(furulya)*. Váralja, Tolna County

Long shepherd's pipe *(hosszú furulya)*. Csurgó, Somogy County

Min-dë- gyik-nek ott a sze-re- tő- je, Csak az e-nyém elmënt messze tőlem.

Réz-sar- kantyúm csak azt csëngi pën-gi: Volt sze-re-tőm el këll fe-lej- te-ni.

In more recent songs, the pentatonic system is even to be found alongside a 'double scheme' (see p. 24).

Szilice (Gömör County), 1913. K.

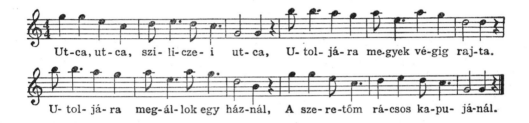

56

Ut-ca, ut-ca, szi- li-cze- i ut- ca, U- tol- já-ra me-gyek vé-gig raj-ta.

U- tol- já- ra meg-ál-lok egy ház-nál, A sze- re-tőm rá-csos ka-pu- já-nál.

Another interesting example is the following AABC construction (Ex. No. 57a). Mari parallel: No. 57b.

Faithful to the facts, the collector recorded the tune as he heard it, with a_1 in the sixth bar. Yet it is quite certain that the melodic structure required b^b_1 at this point. Since the only datum we have is one performance from a single singer *(hapax legomenon)*, fresh data are needed to decide whether this is a chance occurrence, or symptomatic of a general degeneration.

a) *Transylvanian Folksongs:* No. 54. Kászonjakabfalva (Csík County). K.

b) Vasiliev, 1923, No. 44.

57 a

b

Túl a vi- zën ëgy ko- sár Ab- ba sé-tál ëgy ma- dár,

oi ko- re- met, ko- re- met, βüt- šö u- ke, še- re-met!
oi korak so-lat, ko- rak so-lat, iönan üδre-tu- ke, še- re-met!

Ke- rít- ge- tẽm, de nem vár, Jaj Is- te-nẽm de nagy kár.

oị   *pis-te- ret, pis-te- ret,*   *nȃm-ȃš-tet*   *u- ke, še- re-met!*
    tu-lar-žat, tu-la-čȃ-žat,   *a- ra-kat*   *u- ke, še- re-met!*

The next example (Ex. No. 58) shows a Hungarian folk tune, two Chuvash variants and a Rumanian tune (see Note 149). The Chuvash variants prove that the tune is not of Rumanian origin. The final g_1 (a later development) tends to indicate that the Rumanian came from the Hungarian, if they are not of common Kun origin.

a) Hadikfalva (Bukovina), 1914. K., b) Fedorov: *146 Chuvash Folksongs,* Moscow, 1934, No. 100., c) Maximov, No. 121., d) Bartók: *Volksmusik der Rumänen von Maramureş,* No. 34.

58 a   Vé- kon cér- na, ke-méñ ma- ga, Jaj, de' ke- vé le- géñ vagy.

b   *Xo-rȃn šịr-li tɛ- nə- rɛn, Xo-rȃn šịr-li tɛ- nə- rɛn,*

c   *i rɛx tȃ- tȃm i- rak sər, i rɛx tȃ- tȃm i- rak-sər,*

d   *Hai tu mân-dri- o- ru- lé, Hai tu mân-dri- o- ru- lé,*

Fú- nek, fá- nak a- dós vagy, Egy pénz-nek u- ra nem vagy.

ɛp xam šị- sɛ pə- χič- čɛn tut- lȃ mar tɛn- əč- čə.

pị- tɛ śu- rȃm su-pə́ń- sȃr, pị- tɛ śu- rȃm su- pə́ń-sȃr.

Ĵn- do- ie-st'e ju- mă- ta- t'e, Ĵn- do- ie- st'e ju- mă- ta-t'e.

The following well-known Hungarian tune (Mohi [Bars County], 1912, Coll. Z. Kodály; var. Bartók, No. 275a) corresponds to a Chuvash tune (Lach: *Vorläufiger Bericht*, 1918, p. 63, No. 30 given without text; with text, Lach: Chuv. 1940, p. 74, No. 33) widespread in its distribution. For variants see Coll. Maximov, 1932, No. 65; Feinberg: *25 Chuvash Songs*, Moscow, 1937, No. 6.

a) Mohi (Bars County), 1912. K.
b) Lach, 1918, p. 63, No. 30.

The following AABB construction (Exs. Nos. 60, 61) is a relatively rare phenomenon in Hungarian folk material. It has, however, many Mari variants.

Gyergyócsomafalva (Csík County), 1907. B.

a) Lach: Cheremis No. 125.
b) Lach: Wotyak No. 63.
c) Vasiliev, 1920, No. 109.

61 a

b

c

There are further traces in Hungary of pentatonic tunes with *do*-finals: Ex. No. 62.

Bartók, No. 269. Körösfő (Kolozs County), 1907. B.

Tempo giusto

62

Ugy ég a tűz, ha lo- bog,
Ugy é- lek én, ha lo- pok.   Se nem lo- pok, cse- ré- lek,

Még- is i- ga- zán é- lek, I- haj, csu- haj még-is i- ga- zán é- lek.

The remarkable archaic song from Transylvania which follows, arranged for chorus in my *Székely Lament*, has a Chuvash parallel (Coll. Maximov, No. 84).

a) Ph. E. M. No. 1272a. Gyergyószentmiklós (Csík County), 1910. K.

b) Maximov, No. 84.

At present only a few immediate comparisons can be made with the music of other related or adjacent peoples. However, several striking similarities are worthy of mention.

Below, the tune of a folk-ballad from the Zobor district (Ex. No. 64a) is collated with a Wotyak tune (No. 64b published without text).

a) Ph. E. M. No. 1149a. Ghymes (Nyitra County), 1907. K.
b) *Sammelbände der Internationalen Musikgesellschaft* III, p. 437, No. 12.

In the Wotyak example there is the VII ending already mentioned, which in this case is not a final since the tune continues.

The following Nogai-Tartar tune was published in 1901[24]:

There can be no doubt that it is the same as the tune collected by Bartók (Ex. No. 66b). The original notation, given here, is extraordinarily instructive; the Russian collector took the accented short notes for appoggiaturas, just as 'foreign musicians' heard Hungarian folk-rhythms wrongly, with a German ear.[25] It is likely that its rhythm, compared with its Hungarian counterpart, is as follows (Ex. No. 66a):

b) Nagymagyar (Komárom County). B.

Fel van pa-ri- pám nyergel-ve, El- më-he-tek a-kár- mer- re.

The difference in the third line does not affect the identity of the two tunes. The Hungarian tune is living and fairly widespread, and variants showing nearer identity of the third line occur such as the following:

a) AP 3772d. Vállaj (Szatmár County), 1960. L. V.
b) Barlahida (Zala County), 1954. J. Vajda.

67 a

Mi-kor a ju-hász bort i - szik, Szőke sza-már szomor - ko - dik.

Ne szo-mor-kodj sző-ke sza-már! Mindjárt megyünk a nyáj u - tán.

b

É - des-anyám mondta ne-kem, Mi-nek a sze- re - tő ne - kem.

De jén a - ra nem hajoltam, Tit - kon szere-tőt tar - tot - tam.

Equally, a more accurate recording of the Tartar tune might yield a more similar form. The rhythm is identical in both; the first seven syllables of the eight-syllable line are parlando, the last one drawn-out. Also identical are the descending melodic line and the pentatonic scheme (pure in the Tartar, but with three *pien* [extraneous] notes—a_2, e_2, a_1—in the Hungarian). There is no fifth construction (neglecting the slight traces of it in the fourth line of the Hungarian tune), and each of the four lines displays a different melodic content. There are many Hungarian tunes of this type (Ex. No. 68).

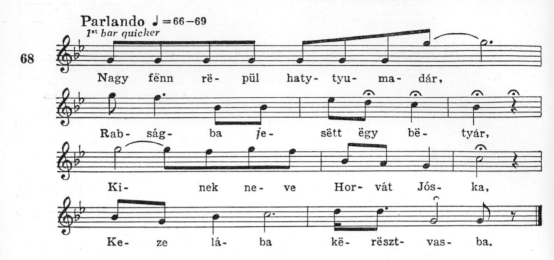

68

Parlando ♩=66—69
1st bar quicker

Nagy fënn rë- pül haty- tyu- ma- dár,

Rab- ság- ba je- sëtt ëgy bë- tyár,

Ki- nek ne- ve Hor- vát Jós- ka,

Ke- ze lá- ba kë- rëszt- vas- ba.

See also Bartók, Nos. 7–32; there are probably other examples amongst the Tartars, too. In default of further data, there is nothing to add about Eastern connections.

We know, however, that the following tune-type is not the property of one or two peoples, but has achieved international currency throughout the East. The Hungarian example was found at Gyergyóújfalu (Csík County), 1910, recorded by Z. Kodály, Ph. E. M., No. 1263a; *Transylvanian Folksongs* No. 83. Its Mari parallel is Lach, No. 70:

a) *Transylvanian Folksongs* No. 83. Ph. E. M. No. 1263a. Gyergyóújfalu (Csík County), 1910. K., b) Lach: Cheremis No. 70.

69 a

Parlando ♩=92

ə Szi- vár-váɲy ha- vas- sán fël-nyőtt roz- ma- ring-szál ə

b

♩=216

šâm ni- jan jə- da- le- təm pi- ᵭəl ᵭa l'ậm

Näm sze- re- ti he- lyit, el- a- kar buj- dos- ni, ə

nâl jol- βan štâ re- təm (?)

Many variants of the first half of this song also occur in Lach's collections of Mordvin, Zyrian and Wotyak songs. The Mongolians sing epic texts to freely improvised and varied forms of it. Even so, it cannot be regarded as a primitive Finno-Ugrian or Turkish type: it seems to embody some more general, supranational, archaic, recitation formula, since these peoples can scarcely have derived it from the liturgical psalms of either the Christian or the Jewish Church, where it still plays a significant role.[26] See, for example, the *Graduale Romanum* (Ratisbonae, 1923, p. 551):

70

This tune can have three kinds of ending (*a, b* or *c*), and is an example of the variability of the final previously mentioned.

Since the germ of pentatonic tunes, and the most frequently occurring groups of notes, are the three neighbouring notes (in our examples b^b, *c, d;* in the first half of double-scheme tunes *f, g, a*), it is easy to imagine the pentatonic scheme arising from a recitation formula of this three-note range. The great mass of primitive examples does not go beyond the range of three notes. They begin on the first (*b^b*), stay on the third (*d_2*) or possibly on the second (*c_2*) for a long time, and end by descending to the first. More developed forms touch the fifth of the opening note (f_2) at one or two strongly accented points (it is a pointer to pentatonic feeling that this is never a fourth); for a more emphatic conclusion, they descend to the lower third of the opening note, g_1, or to its lower fourth, f_1 (Exs. Nos. 71–78).[27]

A. O. Väisänen: *Mordwinische Melodien*, No. 17. Wedding lament.

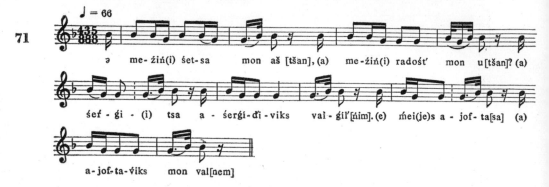

ə me-źiń(i) šet-sa   mon aš [tšan],(a)   me-źiń(i) radošť   mon u[tšan]? (a)

šef-ġi-(i) tsa   a-śergi-ďi-viks   vaı̀-ġil'[ńim].(e)   ḿei(je)s a-jof-ta[sa]   (a)

a-jof-ta-v́iks   mon val[ńem]

ibid. No. 19. Lament.

ńei   mo-n(e)   su-van(i),   mo-n(e) su-van(e)   v́ä-l'ıń

ibid. No. 1. Lyric song.

ďo   ďo-ve   ve-voľ,   ďo-ve   ve-voľ,   ďo   ro-roľ   ďo   ro-roľ(i),   ďo ńeńkaš· ko-roľ,

do-ve   ve-voľ,   do-ve   ve-voľ,   ďo   ro-roľ,   do roro ro-roľ,   ńeńkaš   ko-roľ.

Lach: *op. cit.* (Note No. 14). Wotyak No. 14.

Tö-đe-no Kamlän   šú-ki-ĵez   đa-ri-šän   đa-rä   šukkiš-kä-aı̯-gaı̯!

mi-ľamno kᶒr(e)žam kuara-jos-mᶒ   gurtlänno kuźa-jaz   ӡukkiš-kä-aı̯-gaı̯!

58

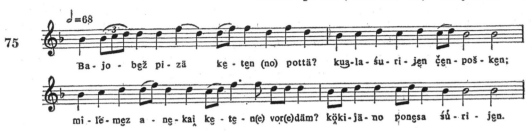

75

Ba - jo - bęž pi - zä   kę - tęn (no) pottä?   kuą-la - śu - ri - jęn čęn - poš - kęn;

mi - lĕ - męz a - nę - kaĮ kę - tę - n(e) voŗ(e)däm? kǫki - jä - no ponęsa śú - ri - jęn.

Lament. CMPH V, No. 199.

76

Parlando rubato ♩=72

ə Édĕsz anyám,   é - dĕsz-a - nyám,   əl - lelkĕm, édĕsz - a - nyám!   ə

♩=120   Hogy tudott ittenyə hagyni min - kĕt,   édĕsz-anyám, ijen   hamaran!   ə

Mámám,   mámám, édĕsz - anyám,   əmmé nem szajnálə   mĕg ingĕ - mĕ   - tə.

mámikám,   mámikám?   etc.

Transylvanian Folksongs No. 56. Gyergyóújfalu (Csík County), 1910. K.

Parlando rubato

77

Ho - va mégy, ho - va mégy   Ti - zĕn - két kő - mi - es? ə

El - mĕ - nyünk, el - mĕ - nyünk,   Hogy - ha dol - got   kap - nánk! (ə)

Bartók, No. 16. Vacsárcsi (Csík County), 1907. B.

Parlando ♪=152

78

Ha ki - indulsz Erdély fe - lől,   Ne   nézz ró - zsám   vissza - fe - lé.

Szivednek ne   lĕgyĕn ne - héz.   Hogy az i - de - gĕn földre mész.

Indeed, f_1g_1-$b\flat_1c_2d_2$-f_2 forms the pentatonic scale. Both the Mari and the Hungarian examples demonstrate a more developed, rhythmically controlled form (which in the Hungarian tunes is linked with a regular number of syllables). Finals descending to f_1 (VII) have already been seen in previous examples. The f_1 of the extra-textual upbeat in the Hungarian example ($\partial = a$ semi-articulated 'neutral' vowel-sound on 'e') appears to be a tenuous vestige of the final on VII.

THE EASTERN ORIGIN
OF THE HUNGARIAN PENTATONIC SYSTEM

To sum up: those Hungarian pentatonic tunes for which Eastern counterparts exist can be divided into three types:

1. The fifth construction: A⁵A⁵AA or A⁵B⁵AB. These are tunes of wide range and in various rhythms, with from six to fifteen syllables—in Hungarian never more than eleven—to the line.

2. The smaller fifth construction, in eight bars, of octave range: A⁵BAB. The construction is related to the previous one, except for the second line in which, after the high opening notes, the tune at once falls to the level of the fourth line. The number of syllables is generally 8, 7, 8, 7, or lines are of the same length: 4×7.

3. Tunes without parallelism (that is, without sections of exactly corresponding content). These move within the narrowest range and usually do not even reach the upper octave. Their range is 1–7 or VII–7, but most frequently ♭3–5 (that is, *do, re, mi*). Many primitive recitation tunes belonging to this group do not even extend beyond the third. Among peoples related to the Hungarians, these tunes all share irregular period construction, a freely varying number of syllables, and prose texts. In Hungary, all examples (with the exception of the lament) have a fixed syllable-count (6–8–12 syllables, see the foregoing musical examples Nos. 71–78, and 69).[28]

Let us see what follows from the aforesaid correspondences.

Basic concepts of musical thought may develop along similar lines among different peoples completely separated from each other. In this way the pentatonic system developed among peoples without mutual contact—African Negroes, North-American Indians, Celts, Chinese, etc. Essential correspondence in melodic construction, phraseology and rhythm, however, is far from accidental. Here, contact or common origin must be assumed. Since such basic elements are found to exist among both Magyars and the existing remnants of Oriental communities from which at some stage the Magyars were derived, it can only be assumed that common elements existed in the community before the Magyars broke away. The Magyars brought them from their old homeland as part of their ancient heritage, along with their language. Today, the Magyars represent the outermost edge of that great Asiatic musical tradition, many thousands of years old, rooted in the spirit of the various peoples who live from China, throughout Central Asia, to the Black Sea.[29]

Despite some changes, the Hungarian language has remained substantially stable; in the same way, Hungarian folk music today is still based on its primitive foundations.

At present, the Ugrian and Turkish elements in Hungarian music cannot be differentiated. This will only be possible when we are more familiar with the music of related peoples, do not have to depend on data recorded by a few amateurs, but can instead draw on the results of exhaustive and methodical research carried out on the spot.[30] Until then, every trait of Hungarian folk music that is unrelated to Western European music, or to the music of our neighbours, must be regarded as Eastern in origin; or else to be a recent autochthonous development springing up from the old roots.

It seems probable that those forms of Hungarian music which resemble Mari and Chuvash material are relics of Old Bulgar influence, to which Hungarian owes some two hundred words. On the evidence of this vocabulary the whole of Magyar life must have been radically transformed between the fifth and seventh centuries, and Magyar music too must have been altered and enriched.

Time may have wiped away the Eastern features from the face of the Magyar community, but in the depth of its soul, where the springs of music lie, there still lives an element of the original East, which links it with peoples whose language it has long since ceased to understand, and who are today so different in mind and spirit.

After exposure to so many foreign influences and to racial admixture, it is amazing that the original musical language of the Magyar community has remained almost intact in at least several hundred tunes. It seems likely that this will continue to remain so. In the following chapter we shall see that, even though the tune-type that preserves the purest form of the Eastern legacy is now dying out, its descendant is to be found in the newer style of tune, now organically flourishing.

III THE NEW STYLE OF FOLKSONG

The tune-type so far considered—we may call it the original stratum—includes approximately two hundred basic tunes, not counting variants. Most of these are known only to old people and are gradually dying out. But this is not so everywhere or all the time; in many places people cling to them with amazing tenacity. Not more than a seventh of this material, however, can today be regarded as known throughout the country. Let us now turn to young people's songs, known by the entire village community. What constitutes that village music which, flourishing on the surface, readily offers itself for research? What is the common speech of modern folk music, the present-day song of present-day people?

The song-repertory contains about 3,000 songs (always excluding variants). Of these, roughly 1,000 are regularly sung, and 800 have a repetitive (reprise) form, with the first line heard again at the end. Setting aside less important types, the main ones have the following musical content: AA^5A^5A, $ABBA$, AA^5BA, $AABA$. Most well-known Hungarian songs belong to one or other of these types. Numerically this is the largest and stylistically most homogeneous group of song, and constant use renders it yet more important.

Superficially, one tune at first seems very much like another, and there is in fact a strong resemblance between them. But this is true in the heyday of every style in every branch of art. It is sufficient to recall the Flemish or Italian schools of painting, and how the style that had been evolved at the hands of leading masters was taken u by nume ous smaller masters, in thousands of artistic products all resembling each other. Again, to quote an example from folk art: at a distance, the embroidered aprons of Mezőkövesd all look alike. But among many thousands, no two are completely identical. The style of present-day Hungarian folksong is fixed and settled in shape and pattern without being rigid; every day new songs are created, but these only differ in detail from those already in existence.

Statistics show the favourite form to be $ABBA$.[31] It is related to the AA^5A^5A type inasmuch as the pitch of B usually corresponds to that of A^5.

B is generally a fifth higher than A. These two forms together account for about sixty per cent of the reprise type.

Neither appears to be frequent in Western-European music,[32] where AABA is more common, though only in recent centuries. Only one out of 147 popular German folksongs of 1530 had this form; it was also rare in French *chansons*, Gregorian music, and troubadour songs.[33] In Hungary, Sebestyén Tinódi (c. 1550) did not know the reprise form. In the Hoffgreff collection, there is only one example of the form ABCA—of Czech origin; and of the 125 melodies in the *Geneva Psalm Book*, only the first psalm illustrates a similar formal principle in its ABCCDA formation. The Harmat–Sík *Szent vagy, Uram!* (Holy art Thou, O Lord, 1933)—the Roman Catholic song-collection that goes back to the earliest sources—contains about thirty specimens of the AABA type. Of these, only one is demonstrably from the seventeenth century, all the rest being of later origin, mostly dating from the end of the eighteenth century. In the light of this evidence, the reprise form, and in particular AABA, has only become more frequent in European music since the sixteenth century. There is no trace of it in Oriental music, so far as is known.[34] It is probable, then, that the Hungarian form has developed under European influence, like its variant, AA⁵BA, the oldest example of which is a fifteenth-century French *chanson*.[35]

79

The repetition of A a fifth higher is perhaps connected with polyphonic music, where the entry of the second voice on the upper fifth is so frequent. The oldest Hungarian example of this is in a manuscript of 1777.[36] The example that follows is one of its modern variants.

a) Ferenc Kovács's manuscript, Hungarian Academy of Sciences.
b) Újszász (Pest County), 1918. B.

80 a

b

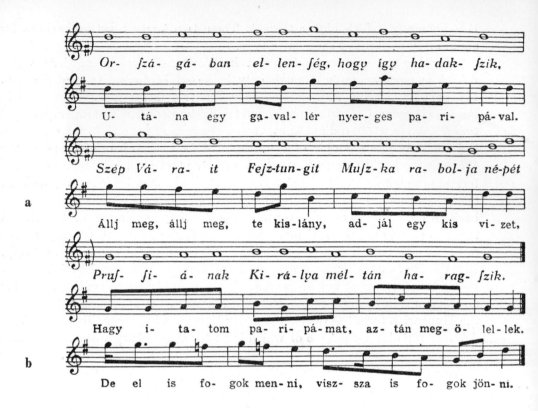

There are many folk variants of this tune, and several minor versions also. The last line of Ex. No. 80 is the third one from a different variant resembling the MS. more closely. An especially interesting Transdanubian variant is shown below. Here a few characteristic Transdanubian pentatonic features (tritone-phrasing at line-endings) have penetrated a tune that originally was doubtless a purely major melody.

Nagybajom (Somogy County), 1922. K.

81

This type was previously regarded as the dominant type of Hungarian folksong, probably because popular art-songs made frequent use of it.

Playing the long shepherd's pipe *(hosszú furulya)*. Somogy County

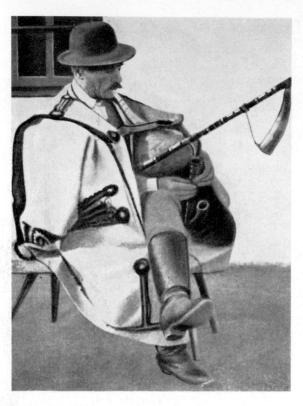

Palócman, inhabitant of Northern Hungary, playing the bagpipe. Environs of Szécsény, Nógrád County

Bagpiper from Buják, Nógrád County

The following tune (Ex. No. 82a) from Csík County (*Transylvanian Folk-songs* No. 132) is essentially the same as the 'Schweizerlied' (Ex. No. 82b) made known through Beethoven's Variations, and thus is certainly of German origin.[37] It is also closely related to the French *chanson* (see p. 63, Ex. No. 79).

a) *Transylvanian Folksongs* No. 132. Gyergyóújfalu (Csík County), 1910. K.

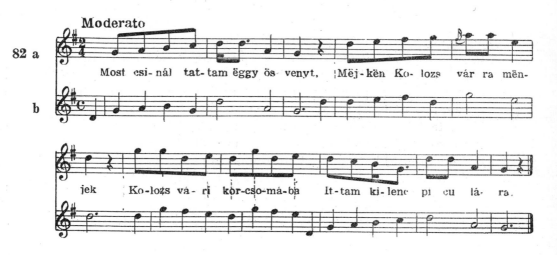

Such closeness of identity in form and material with German tunes is uncommon, but the formal principle is unquestionably European in origin. Its spread in Hungary has been fostered by sacred and secular tunes brought from abroad, and through the medium of art-songs that developed in their wake. Owing to the lack of research into the history of form, the age and development of this principle cannot be established in greater detail. It is not as yet known whether its first appearance was on French or German soil. The German tune and the French *chanson* are in any case variations on the same basic type; they even agree in the 'tonal answer' of the second tune-line. The Hungarian version can scarcely be more than two, or two and a half centuries old.

In any case, the most common and characteristic types of this new song stratum of Hungarian tunes are not the Western-European AABA or AA⁵BA types, but ABBA and its close relative AA⁵A⁵A. In these, too, the principle of the first line returning at the end may have come from the West. They exhibit, however, another characteristic which leads to believe that they are more closely related to the original stratum than had hitherto been realized.

CONNECTIONS BETWEEN
THE NEW SONG FORM AND THE OLD

It is very rare for a tune to be sung once only: once begun, it is repeated several times at a stretch, though not necessarily in the old style of Hungarian merrymaking, when a single song was played and sung the whole night long. Thus the listener hears not AA⁵A⁵A, but the following:

$$A^5A^5 \qquad A^5A^5 \qquad A^5A^5$$
$$A \qquad AA \qquad AA \qquad A...$$

—that is to say, not isolated stanzas, but continuous interrelated musical transpositions. Omit the first A, and the old Hungarian–Mari fifth construction appears. Thus the old form A⁵A⁵AA may easily have been changed to AA⁵A⁵A, even without European influence. The four-line stanza needed only one chance setting to a different tune-line; there was no need to interrupt the tune, even if the text used up a later line. Even now, when a poorish singer makes a mistake or omits a text-line he continues unhesitatingly, even though the fourth tune-line has to be transferred to the first line of the following verse. When the text ends, the song stops, even if it is in the middle of the tune. The mistake is perpetuated and a new form is available. Similar displacement has caused many Hungarian ABBA tunes to appear as AABA in variants. In Bartók: *Népzenénk és a szomszéd népek népzenéje* (Our Folk Music and the Folk Music of Neighbouring Peoples; Berlin–Leipzig, W. de Gruyter, Ung. Bibl. Vol. I) examples (p. 13 and Ex. No. 16) reveal that when the Hungarian ABBA type is adopted by Slovaks, it can also assume the form BBAA (Exs. Nos. 83, 84 and 85).

Bartók: *Népzenénk...* (Our Folk Music...) No. 16. Mezőköz (Zólyom County), 1915. B.

P. Járdányi: *Magyar népdaltípusok*, 1961, II, 93. Prevalent throughout the country.

Tempo giusto

84

Sej haj, a mj házunk sár-gá-ra van me-szel-ve.

O - da - jár a cim-bal-mos úr min-dën szomba - ton es - te.

Mindig csak azt cim-bal-mŏz-za cim-bal-má-val fü - lem - be:

Sej haj, gon-dolj kislány a ré - gi sze - re - tőd - re!

Ibid. 125. Prevalent throughout the country.

Tempo giusto

85

Kint a fa - lu szé-lén kék në-fe-lejts nyí - lik.

Lë - szë - dëm, lë - szö-dëm, a - kár - meny-nyi nyí - lik.

Lë - szë - dëm, lë - szö-dëm, jus - sak az e - szëd - be.

Rá së gon - do - lok a ré - gi sze - re - tőm - re.

Ex. No. 84 lies closer to the Slovak tune with its line B, and No. 85 with its line A.

Apart from this displacement of text, purely musical factors may account for morphological changes. There is, for example, a singular Mari tune-type, of which at the moment but few examples are known (Ex. No. 86). Further examples are: Lach, No. 91 and its variants 83, 88. (Ph. E. M. Nos. 620c, 621a.)

Tempo giusto

86

(There is no text)

On the phonograph-cylinder, the fourth line is at the pitch of the first, but Mari tune-construction would normally make the fourth line a fifth lower than the second (see Note 19). The tune could be written in letters $A^8A^5A^5A$. Recently, a novice collector noted down a well-known Hungarian tune with the same form.

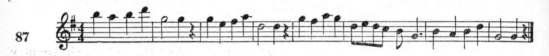

87

If the third line is regarded as a modified A^5, the formula is again $A^8A^5A^5A$. Normally the first and fourth lines are at the same pitch, and a more experienced collector would probably have considered the unexpected pitch of the first line as a chance aberration, and would have written it down in the lower octave. In view of the Mari examples (see Ex. No. 86), and the descending tendency of Hungarian tune-lines, it may well be that this was indeed the primitive form of some Hungarian tunes before it changed to AA^5A^5A; the uncomfortably high first line was thus shifted an octave lower, to the same pitch as the fourth. In songs of wider range, peasant singers tend to do this for themselves even now.[38] Thus the new form may have been the result of autochthonous development. This hypothesis would be corroborated, were variants of the following Chuvash tune to become known. So far it is unique:

Fedorov, 1934, No. 34.

88

However, an example exists among the Chuvash tunes reminiscent of the form AA^5A^5A.

The archaic tonal system, and the old formal principle, are both functional in new-type Hungarian songs. Most of them appear to be heptatonic scales (Dorian, Aeolian, Mixolydian and even modern major); but if subsidiary, unstressed notes are omitted, and characteristic turns observed, the basic pentatonic series generally emerges clearly. To apply the names of the church modes to such tunes is inaccurate, since their lilt and phrasing are totally different from church melodies, many of which are also purely pentatonic. Hence it is possible to say, with some reservations, that the pentatonic scale is the most characteristic scale in the new Hungarian melodic style as well.

The following tune is pentatonic; its form is AA⁵A⁵A: 1906, Coll. Z. Kodály:

Zabar (Gömör County), 1906. K.

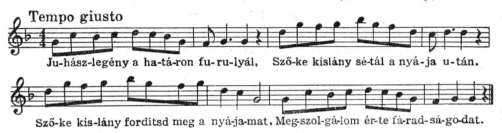

Upper *b♭* corresponds to the *d* falling on the fifth syllable, a regular characteristic of Mari–Chuvash single-scheme tunes. (For the substitution of the sixth, see Note 19.) The following two examples also exhibit pure pentatonic scales.

Csurgónagymarton (Somogy County), 1922. K.

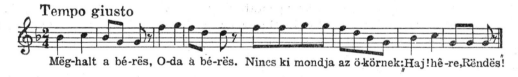

Bolhás (Somogy County), 1922. K.

The unusual rhythm of the latter is reminiscent of a medieval hymn form, but no direct connection is known to exist.[39]

If the first line of these tunes is transposed an octave higher, the **Mari** type mentioned above (No. 86) is obtained.

In a few, only one extraneous note occurs: in the final figure of an eleven-syllable line,

92

in which the original g_1

93

was raised to a, simply perhaps as a result of stronger emphasis. This is the most frequent line-ending of the old-style, pentatonic, eleven-syllable tune, although a sometimes creeps in here, too. (See Ex. No. 27.)[40]

If the song is interpreted as a double-scheme tune, the upper a_2 does not appear to be an extraneous note:

Bolhás (Somogy County), 1922. K.

94

In any case, the clearly pentatonic character of the tune is not invalidated, either by this note or by the Dorian or Aeolian sixth.[41] This is illustrated by the following example, sung by a nineteen-year-old hussar:

Nyírvaja (Szabolcs County), 1916. K.

95

In form it is Dorian; in essence, pentatonic. The middle lines, as shown by the interval relationship above the first line, and by the square notes, are still close enough to the others to be regarded as minor deviants from A^5, halfway between A and B. At the end of the third tune-line, an attractive extension relieves the monotony that would arise were the two middle lines identical. Here is a closely related variant differing in form sung by young soldiers.

Szilágyperecsen (Szilágy County), 1916. K.

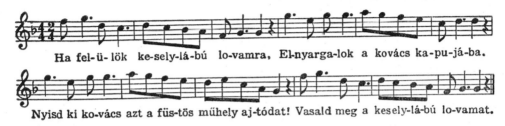

Ha fel-ü-lök ke-sely-lá-bú lo-vamra, El-nyarga-lok a kovács ka-pu-já-ba.

Nyisd ki ko-vács azt a füs-tös műhely aj-tódat! Vasald meg a kesely-lá-bú lo-vamat.

The first and last lines are so purely pentatonic, and the *so-la* cadence so particularly characteristic of pentatony,[42] that the more adventurous wanderings of the middle lines do not rob the tune of its pentatonic character. A third variant of this tune is sung with a major third in the middle:

Zsére (Nyitra County), 1911. K.

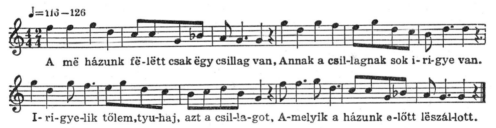

A më házunk fë-lëtt csak ëgy csillag van, Annak a csil-lagnak sok i-ri-gye van.

I-ri-gye-lik tőlem,tyu-haj, azt a csil-la-got, A-melyik a házunk e-lőtt lëszál-lott.

These three variants throw some light on the nature of folksong variation. With some slight exaggeration, it may be said that twenty or thirty tunes can be placed side by side so that there will hardly be any difference between any two adjacent tunes, and scarcely any similarity between the first and last.

Two further variants bring the tune so close to major and minor tonality, respectively, that only a few traces of the pentatonic scale remain: namely, the three-note group d_2, f_2, g_2 in the first, and the phrase $g_2a_2g_2c_2d_2g_2f_2$ in the middle line of the second (Exs. Nos. 98–99):

Baracska (Fejér County), 1911. B.

Éj-fél u-tán egy-gyet ü-tött az ó-ra. Gye-re ba-bám ki-sér-jél ki jaz út-ra!

Ki-ki-sér-lek, ki jaz út-nak sej,kö-ze-pé-re, Meg-ö-lellek,megcsókollak kedvemre.

In dance-step

99

Ha még ëgyszër tü-zes mén-kű lë-hetnék, I-polynyé-ki so-ro-zó-ba be-üt-nék.

A-gyon-ütném i-polynyé-ki csu-haj! i-ro-dát, A le-gényëk szive szomo-rí-tó-ját.

The new Hungarian melody-style is thus an organic continuation of the old. It retains—though in changed forms—both main principles: the pentatonic system and the fifth construction. Line by line, the shape of a tune has changed: A⁵A⁵AA is replaced by AA⁵A⁵A and its variants. But the principle is essentially the same and involves the symmetrical interchange of two higher and two lower lines. Construction apart, the tonal system of the old style, the pentatonic, lives on in the new songs, sometimes in complete purity, sometimes hidden under multifarious heptatonic scales, its traces more or less visible. The tenacity with which the pentatonic system persists testifies, moreover, to the fact that for Hungarians it has always been the instinctive means of musical expression. This is why it has not been suppressed by European influences, by assimilation, by racial mixing, etc., any more than by the more recent influence of art-song, imbued to a greater or lesser degree with foreign elements.

THE INFLUENCE OF POPULAR ART-SONG

What was this influence? In the absence of exhaustive analysis, a few general observations must suffice. How it came about is quite clear. The production of art-songs between 1850 and 1900 flooded the Hungarian countryside, and the peasantry adopted certain of the new songs. Some of the authors have not been traced, for the songs were published anonymously or under several different names. Many of the best and most characteristic tunes known to peasant singers will never be traced back to their authors.

This half century was a productive period for folksong also. Many tunes, without counterparts in older collections, suddenly appeared, and their style could not be attributed to known composers of the day. Nor could they have originated at the hands of unknown, but well-equipped composers, for they reveal an entirely different cast of mind. The art-song tends to reflect the spirit of the flagging middle class and the disappearing gentry, in the darkened emotional atmosphere of the late-romantic and post-revolutionary period.

That is why it is pervaded by hopeless resignation. (It would indeed be worth while making a serious study of the psychological background of these art-songs and of their poetic, stylistic and technical development.) The village people, on the contrary, the people of Kossuth, were teeming with life, and were still hopeful and optimistic even after so much disillusionment; they voice this in their songs. Even though they adopted and developed new forms from certain art-songs, they generally stood firm by their own old tradition and evolved it still further. The generation that adopted these songs was followed by that born after 1890; and a decided revolution in style occurred, as if the new generation had grown tired of the many popular art-songs heard for a lifetime from its parents. The new folksong was a reaction against a weakening life-force, against endless, aimless grief and longing for death. Instead of soft, languishing melodies in the minor, and tripping, twittering tunes in major keys, the vigorous, monumental voice of the grandfathers rings out again. The flood of town songs was not able to tune the folksong to the pitch of their own torpid and mawkish laments. All that happened was that here and there its means of expression was enriched as a result of contact. It must, however, be stressed that middle-class songs had become increasingly more Magyarized and popular since the introduction of the foreign style, described as 'noble folksongs' by K. Szini (1865); this process continued up to the time of Dankó's songs (1858–1903). The more the new art-music resembled folk-tradition, the more its influence spread amongst the peasants.

As for rhythmic influence: while the folksongs written down before the eighties are shorter, consisting of lines with six to twelve syllables, the lines of the new songs—certainly under the influence of the long and more complex art-songs—may have as many as twenty-five syllables.

In tonality, modern major and minor may temporarily have had a stronger influence, but have not lastingly influenced the majority. Today's folksongs, if not pentatonic, are either Dorian, Aeolian or Mixolydian. Frequently, when sung by peasant singers, the characteristic minor idioms of borrowed art-songs turned into Dorian, Aeolian, and even pentatonic idioms. It is illuminating to follow the fate of the semitone. The pure pentatonic system does not, of course, recognize the semitone interval. Hungarians probably became aware of the interval of the diatonic semitone only after they had settled in their present homeland; the exact date cannot be fixed, although it was probably late. Indeed, among peoples retaining the pure five-note system, even the auxiliary ornamental notes come from within the system, as though other notes did not exist. Korean children being educated in Hungary in 1960 learned the diatonic semitone with great difficulty, if at all.

Nowadays, Hungarians are completely at home with heptatonic scales, but they have not adopted the chromatic semitone from art-songs. Whenever they come across it, they simplify it. In schools and choirs, individuals learn such stylistic devices, but, generally speaking, the chromatic semitone does not belong to the peasants' tonal system even today.

Here is an example of how peasant singers treat a tune taken 'from above.' The melody (Ex. No. 100a) first appeared about 1877. It is quoted in the form in which it appears in a collection of 1900.[43] The folk variant (No. 100b) is from Tolmács (Nógrád County): 1921, Coll. Z. Kodály.

The original AA⁵BA has turned into ABBA, so that the second line connects with the first more naturally; there is no leap of a seventh. The diminished fifth (marked 'Nb') has become a fourth, owing to the difficulty of singing it. True, the tune has thereby lost an expressive though somewhat sensitive climax, but the diminished fifth is as foreign an interval to folk singers as is the chromatic semitone or any other augmented or diminished interval. In folk music, the so-called Hungarian scale *(g-a♭-b-c-d-e♭-f♯-g)* is unknown. It is somewhat rare to hear a descending augmented second; it usually occurs with fluctuating intonation in tunes of foreign origin. Other intervals are always used with great selectivity. Thus the ascending major sixth is rare, as also is the minor seventh—the major never occurs—and they are heard even less frequently as descending intervals. The more common ascending octave and minor sixth are fairly rare as descending intervals. In this tune (No. 100) the folk variant has eliminated the descending minor sixth of the first and fourth lines. All that remains is the major and minor second, the third, the perfect fourth and fifth, both ascending and descending, and the ascending minor sixth and octave. This is indicative neither of poverty nor primitiveness. Every great classical style is characterized by limitation rather than profusion in its artistic means. In its choice of intervals, Hungarian folksong agrees almost entirely with the two peaks in melodic evolution, namely, Gregorian chant, and the melodic style of Palestrina. In both cases, we are confronted with a unison melody-style conceived without need of vocal harmony. Despite its polyphonic matrix, Palestrina's melodic line never belies its monophonic character.[44] In Hungarian folk music, the choice of intervals is strongly influenced by pentatonic feeling, still very much alive today.

The influence of art-music is almost always responsible for the presence of exceptional intervals. But the previous example (No. 100) shows how the folk environment reacts against this, and how it endeavours to reshape art-song to its own pattern. It can happen that 'folkified' art-songs become caricatures; but generally, as in this example, reshaping is not detrimental. That folk usage has a smoothing and polishing effect on text and tune alike, is eloquently attested by innumerable examples.

However, the influence of art-song can sometimes impoverish as well as enrich. Although the old songs would in any case have disappeared with the passage of time, it is certain that the art-song hastened this process with its implications of the new and the fashionable. It also contributed to the decay of ornamentation. Even in the middle of the last century, true folksongs were occasionally published with *melismata*, which were still more frequent in the art-songs of the first half of this century. (The 'folksong composers' of the day—such as Szerdahelyi, Egressy, Füredi—were opera singers.) Later Hungarian art-songs became increasingly syllabic, and ornamentation disappeared from the folksong collections (Bartalus!). Increasingly, fault was found with gipsy flourishes, and with the over-ornamented songs of village church-cantors and old peasant women. Period taste for simplification—which reached a climax in the colourless version of the 'Szózat' (regarded as the second national anthem)—eliminated *melismata* from the newer folksong.

From many points of view this meant impoverishment. We are forced to the conclusion that vocal standards of folk singing have greatly declined: a hundred years ago it would have been usual to hear beautifully ornamented, melismatic singing, not only from individuals, but from groups as well; by 1910, it had become rare to hear such singing, even from old people. The taste for simplification revolted against the more complex style of performance, and singing sank to a more primitive level. Less vocal ability is required for the modern syllabic song, and although singing is taught in schools nowadays, it does not reach the standard that prevailed when it was not taught. Another difference is that performance has lost something of its emotional power and lyric warmth. In the tame syllabic songs of today, scarcely differing in tone from ordinary conversation, there is far less lyrical fervour than, for instance, in the highly-ornamented, melismatic outpourings of an old Székely's complaint. Particularly in Transylvania, the old people sang with much variety of vocal timbre, under the pressure of emotions both solemn and gay, using a different tone from that of everyday conversation, and a different position of the larynx.

If the singing of young people today differs at all from speech, it does so in volume, which is always maintained at the same level; in the old singing style, traces of dynamic variation could still be heard.

The few two-note *melismata* and *portamenti* that have survived as last traces of the old ornamentation show that singing cannot dispense with them. The number of such elements seems to be on the increase in young people's songs, indicating perhaps a coming change in folk taste.

IV CHILDREN'S SONGS AND 'REGÖS' SONGS

In games and round dances, children sing rhythmic folksongs in time with their feet; these derive from the songs of adults. Typical children's songs, and the closely related 'regös' songs, are completely different in form and content from most folksongs. (The Hungarian 'regölés,' 'regös ének' are ancient New Year greetings, formerly associated with ancient fertility rites.) All the children's songs in this category seem to be either variations on, or larger or smaller fragments of, one basic tune. Their scale is formed from the first six degrees of the major scale: g_1-a_1-b_1-c_2-d_2-e_2, the Indo-European hexachord.[45] This is so familiar that it can be identified even from a few notes.

Some of the short children's chants have only two notes:[46]

101

Csi- ga, bi- ga, gye- re ki, *etc*

Countless analogies prove that this is not a fragment of a scale starting on *a*, but the third and second notes of the hexachord, as is at once evident in a three-note variant:[47]

102

Csi- ga, bi- ga, gye- re ki, *etc.*

Two notes forming a minor third are clearly the third and fifth,[48] even without a leap to the tonic at the end, such as occurs in another variant.[49]

103

Csi- ga, bi- ga tóld ki szar-va-dat

This is even clearer when the sixth is added.[50] This phrase is nearly pentatonic and perhaps derives from that system.

Tö- ri, tö- ri sós-ka,
Zsi- dó le-gény csontja.

This may be compared with other tunes that consist of the outer notes with the middle ones lacking.[51] Tunes made up of the notes *a-b-c* contain the second, third and fourth notes of the hexachord, not the first three notes of a minor scale.[52]

In rare cases, the hexachord is extended, and reaches down to the leading note[53] or even to the lower fifth.[54] In the other direction, it is extended to f[55] (influenced perhaps by certain Mixolydian tunes[56]) and, more rarely, reaches g_2.[57]

All this does not alter the tune's hexachordal character any more than the presence of the major seventh does.[58] Nor is the feeling of the hexachord destroyed if the tune occasionally uses the augmented fourth as a passing-note.[59]

The basic rhythmical form of children's songs is the two-bar motif:

This corresponds to two dance-steps, the right and left foot moving alternately on the stressed beats, while the other foot closes up on the unaccented beat. In round-dances, when the dancers are moving in one direction, the same leg always moves with the accented beat. The text has a minimum of three syllables:

but this can be freely varied by division, and may be increased to nine syllables in all.

The simplest children's songs (see the above examples) are of two bars only, and sometimes even these are formed by the repetition of a single bar.[60] The two bars are repeated for the length of the text. A three-bar motif is rare,[61] but in longer songs a second, third or even fourth pair of bars appears, and the song approaches the outward form of the regular four-line construction.[62] The best example of this is 'Erdő mellett nem jó lakni' (It is not good to live near a wood)[63] but the frequent repetition of the pairs of bars sharply distinguishes this type from true quatrains.

In the few tunes that do not conform to the hexachordal system, there are traces of snatches of other tunes.[64] Such familiar melodies generally play a distinctive role in children's songs. Fragments of 'grown-up songs' can occasionally be heard in diminished paraphrases, as if the tune were being broken up into its component parts, by the two-beat lilt of children's songs. Its outlines are still visible, but the basic structure is distorted and broken.

78

Thus in Ex. No. 108 (first published by Áron Kiss's *Magyar gyermek-játék-gyűjtemény* [Collection of Hungarian Children's Games], p. 431, No. 9; and recently CMPH Vol. I, No. 984) there can still be seen the faded outlines of an art-song, 'Húzzad csak, húzzad csak keservesen' (Play on into sadness) (Ex. No. 109a), made known through the medium of the folk play: *A falu rossza*. Here the construction has remained intact, and only the rhythm and melody have been simplified, so that it is almost a variant. This process was facilitated by the old form of eight-syllable bagpipe tunes (Ex. No. 109b).

Borsosberény (Nógrád County), 1937. L.

108

Zi - bit   za - bot   a   lo - vá - nak, Gyöngyöt gyöngyöt asz-szo - nyá-nak.

Gyöngyko - szo -rút   a   lá - nyá-nak, Haj-lós   pál-cát   a   fi - á - nak.

109 a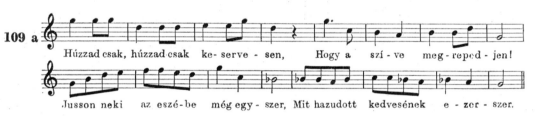

Húzzad csak, húzzad csak ke - serve - sen,   Hogy a   szí - ve   meg - reped - jen!

Jusson neki   az eszé-be   még egy - szer, Mit hazudott kedvesének   e - zer - szer.

b

Tempo giusto ♩ = 138

Pis- ta   bá - csi,   Já- nos bá- csi, Csak a   lá - dám,   azt vi-gyék ki.

Vi- gyék   ki   a   kis kert mö- gé, Hogy on-nan el   ne   vi - hes-sék.

Another song has fragments of the once popular 'Angyal Bandi'[65] which in its complete form exists as a New Year greeting-song.[66] For further examples, see CMPH Vol. I. Several children's songs include a small section of the popular 'Nem ettem én ma egyebet' (I haven't eaten anything else today). (See Kiss: *op. cit.*, p. 422, lines 5 and 10; CMPH Vol. I, p. 387, lines 6 and 11.)

Another has part of 'Kerek ez a zsemle' (This bun is round). (Kiss: *op. cit.*, p. 151; and CMPH Vol. I, No. 1111, last bars.) The material for the Collection of Hungarian Children's Games (Á. Kiss: *Magyar gyermekjáték-gyűjtemény*, 1891) was compiled in 1885 and the song fragments it contains were popular songs of the day to be heard throughout the country. The remains of more recent well-known songs can still be similarly traced in children's songs.

Collectors do not usually consider such things worth recording, yet it is the best way of observing how musical material is worked and shaped in children's consciousness. Some examples clearly show how the adult tune is bent, twisted and ground down when children adopt it, since to them rhythm matters above everything else. (Kiss: *op. cit.*, p. 277, lines 4–6; CMPH Vol. I, p. 563.) In their first imitative attempts at singing, even young children can copy rhythm correctly, though they cannot manage to follow pitch variations since their voices are unable to leap the larger intervals. Our example No. 110, a variant of a tune in Bartók's collection (No. 245), is to be found in a broken form in Kiss: *op. cit.*, p. 277, last five lines; and in Ex. No. 111.

Egyházashetye (Vas County). K.

110

Tempo giusto

Meg- fog- tam egy szu- nyo- got, na-gyobb volt egy ló-nál,
Ki- sü- töt- tem a zsir-ját, több volt egy a- kó-nál.

A- ki ez- tet el- hi- szi, sza- ma- rabb a ló-nál,

A- ki ez- tet el- hi- szi, sza- ma- rabb a ló-nál.

CMPH I, No. 645 (Kiss, p. 398, No. 12).

111

Szé- na al - ja, szé- na al - ja, szé- na sza- ka - dék - ja,

ben- ne va - gyon ke - rék asz - szony, ke-rék kis me - nyecske.

Las- san, könnyen, csak csen - de - sen, ö-leld, a-kit sze-retsz.
Ezt ö - le - lem, ezt ked - ve - lem, komámasszony lá - nyát.
Ezt Ka - ti - cát, ezt Na - ni - cát, szinű, szinű ró - zsát.

80

Recruiting *(verbunkos)*. The bagpiper is playing in the foreground, while the new recruit dances between two recruiting soldiers. They have already put a shako on his head and buckled on his sword. (A drawing of 1816)

Bagpipe-heads from Szeged City Museum

Hurdy-gurdy *(nyenyere)* from Szentes, open

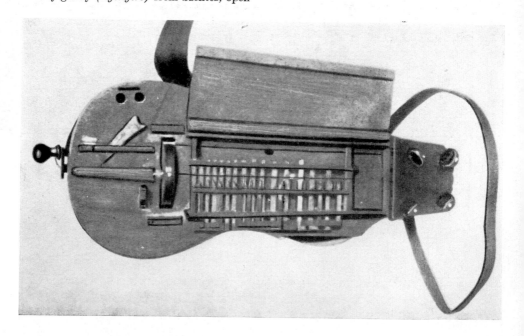

A fe - jem - re tet - tem gyöngyös ko - sa - ra - mat.
Ne híj - ja - tok en - gem Tu - bi I - lo - ná - nak,
csak híj - ja - tok en - gem vi - lág szép lá - nyá - nak,

mert én va - gyok asz - szo - nyomnak fo - gadott le - á - nya.
sej, Du - ná - nak, tu - li - pán - nak gyönyörű vi - rág - ja.

két kis kecske jár - ja, mégis szépen jár - ja. Adjon Isten csendes essőt, Ju - lis - ka,
hadd mossa el mind a kettőt Ma - ris - ka,

Ju - lis - ka is gon - dos - ko - dik én ró - lam is i - dább is,
o dább is.

Ég a gyer - tya, sej, azt a lá - nyok szé - pen jár - ják!
ha meg - gyújt - ják,

The same process occurs in the 'regös' songs (or carols). Whenever an exception occurs, it is a corrupt transformation of a widespread song (see for instance the variant of No. 110 in the *Regös Song* volume of the Kisfaludy Társaság, No. 19). The rest are all hexachordal tunes. This type normally begins on the fifth or on an adjacent note, and its chief characteristic is an upward leap of a fifth to the unaccented beat of the even bars. This interval occurs in practically every 'regös' song, though in some variants leaps of a

Cséb (Zala County). S.

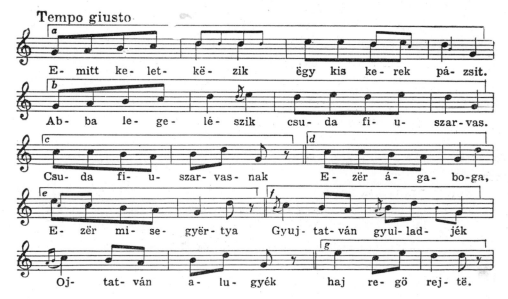

Tempo giusto

E - mitt ke - let - kë - zik ëgy kis ke - rek pá - zsit.

Ab - ba le - ge - lé - szik csu - da fi - u - szar - vas.

Csu - da fi - u - szar - vas - nak E - zër á - ga - bo - ga,

E - zër mi - se - gyër - tya Gyuj - tat - ván gyul - lad - jék

Oj - tat - ván a - lu - gyék haj re - gö rej - të.

(a) Azt is mëgengedtë de *ja* nagy úristen.
(f) Hét ökör, régi törvény, (*g*) Haj regö rejtë.
(a) Kel fő, kel fő házigazda, (*g*) Haj regö rejtë.
(a) Szállott isten házadra, (*g*) Haj regö rejtë,
(f) Népével, seregével, (*e*) teli poharával, (*e*) vetëtt asztalával.
(a) Azt is mëgengedtë de *ja* nagy úristen, (*g*) Haj regö rejtë.
(a) Csattos erszén a derekán, (*g*) Haj regö rejtë.
(c) Abba vagyon száztíz garas, (*g*) Haj regö rejtë.
(c) Felë szeginy regösöké, (*d*) Felë a gazdájé, (*g*) Hej regö rejtë.
(c) Csiszegünk, csoszogunk, (*c*) cserfakéreg bocskorunk

Haj- di- na   pël- va   kön- tö- sünk,   zab nad- rá- gunk.

fourth or a sixth occur (a fourth in CMPH Vol. I, Nos. 857–858 and 859, and a sixth in No. 853, *ibid.*). In children's songs the downward leap of a fifth is generally more common, but the upward leap of a fifth (sometimes a fourth) exists as well. (Upward leap of a fifth: Kiss, pp. 360 and 461; CMPH Vol. I, pp. 487, 507, 555, 558, 540, 549; upward leap of a fourth: Kiss, p. 401; CMPH Vol. I, p. 790.) This is yet another common characteristic of 'regös' songs and children's songs.

Gyenesdiás (Zala County). S.

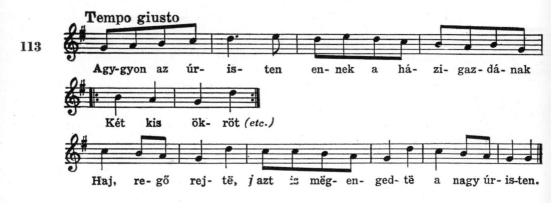

Tempo giusto

113

Agy-gyon az   úr- is- ten   en- nek   a   há- zi- gaz- dá- nak

Két   kis   ök- röt *(etc.)*

Haj,   re- gő   rej- të,   *j* azt   is   mëg- en- ged- të   a   nagy úr- is- ten.

Kénos (Udvarhely County), 1903. V.

Moderato

114

Por- ka   ha-vak   e- se- dëz-nek,   de   hó   re-me,   ró- ma.

115

Tempo giusto

Në fuss, në fuss, në fuss szent Ist- ván ki- rá- lyunk,

mi sëm va- gyunk ör- dö- gök, ha- nëm a te szol- gá- id:

Haj, re- gö raj- ta, azt is meg- ad- hat- ja az a nagy úr- is- ten.

Ad- jon az úr- is- ten en- nek a gaz- dá- nak

két hold fő- det, száz kë- rëszt bú- zát, haj re- gö raj- ta,

azt is mëg- ad- hat- ja az a nagy úr- is- ten.

Further examples will be found in CMPH Vol. II, pp. 776–876.

Ferenc Xaver Kuhac[67] tried to prove that Hungarian 'regös' songs were of Croatian origin. But his examples prove precisely the opposite; and he failed to demonstrate any convincing relationship. It is more probable that some of the hexachordal tunes originate from pentatonic tunes. In the music of peoples related to the Hungarians, there are many tunes with a six-note range which seem to be hexachordal; but as they always lack the fourth and seventh, they may also be regarded as pentatonic (*do-re-mi-so-la*, final note *do*, or *so-la-do-re-mi*, final note *so*). (See Ex. No. 75.) There are also one or two Hungarian examples of this kind, suggesting that in other Hungarian hexachords, too, *fa* is only a later acquisition.

CMPH II, No. 855.

116

Ê- re lőt- ték füöd-nek nyo- mát, Ki há- za ez? Jám- bor- ej- jé,
Jám- bor em- bér la- kik ben- né.

Refr.

Hej, re- gő rej- tém, rej- tém.

Nevertheless, 'regös' songs and children's songs seem to belong to a wider human community. Wherever hexachordal tunes occur, primarily among the Germans and Slavs, pairs of bars related to the Hungarian can be found. The tunes in F. M. Böhme's *Kinderlied und Kinderspiel* (1893) constantly resemble Hungarian children's songs. The form itself spreads over an even wider area. The endless repetition of pairs of bars, or of short motifs in general, is characteristic of the music of all primitive peoples, and even of Gregorian psalm-tunes. In their songs, as in their whole development, children re-enact the primitive life of man, and this is why they begin their musical life with the primitive form of repeating motifs.

V LAMENTS

Mourning songs for the dead go back to primitive times. Although every religion and even secular forms of legislation (for example, Solon's) have endeavoured to control mourning practices, they are still customary even today. In some places, especially among southern peoples, they are accompanied by such intense outbreaks of grief that they cannot be very different from the unrestrained lamentations of primitive man.[68] There is no evidence of such vehemence among the more restrained Hungarians, but it is hardly credible how large a territory still shows traces of mourning ceremonies, and in how many places they are still practised. They are difficult to witness, because their existence is denied, and nothing will persuade people to perform before strangers. It is useless for the collector to attend funerals, for as soon as he is noticed, the mourning ceremonies are omitted, even where they are normally practised. All collectors agree that noting mourning songs is a most difficult undertaking.[69] Few data were available for this reason.[70]

In Hungary—and wherever mourning ceremonies exist or have been practised in the past—the task of mourning falls to women,[71] and in particular to the nearest female relative. People watch the performance carefully and discuss it afterwards: 'She wailed beautifully,' 'She hasn't even mourned for him,' etc. They criticize the mourner if her sincerity is open to doubt, or if she has not come up to expectations.

The spread of civilization gradually makes every display of human emotion, mourning included, more sober and more impersonal. Where the majority regard lamenting as old-fashioned and antiquated, it is the object of ruthless scorn and mockery. Poetic ability does not come to everyone in equal measure; and while even the cynic listens with respect when genuine grief calls forth some magnificent improvisation, the unsophisticated naiveties and occasional puerilities of some unsuccessful though sincere 'necrologist' will at times provoke coarse parodies. These are frequently remembered long after the original laments have sunk into oblivion.

Here and there one hears rumours of paid mourners, but I have never encountered them, nor is there any reliable information about their existence.[72] When I first succeeded in hearing laments, they were nearly always caused by genuine sorrow. That is why there are no complete and faultless texts; during most of the recordings the singers burst into tears and were unable to continue. Though some of the more successful give some idea of the music, the text can only be taken down in shorthand after an actual mourning ceremony with the corpse already buried (when the music would be lacking). No singer could recite a mourning song twice without variation, so entirely does it depend on the inspiration of the moment. That is why the texts of recorded laments in Hungary are less colourful than the actual performance. Another trouble was that phonograph cylinders lasted only two minutes, and even discs only lasted three to four minutes. The beginning was usually wasted while the mourner warmed to her task, and the end came before she was properly in her stride, for such women could recite for half an hour at a stretch. This difficulty has been overcome by the introduction of tape recording. Laments recorded by this means are published in CMPH Vol. V.

On one occasion I wished to hear a woman's lament before recording it. It was extremely beautiful. She immediately repeated it in front of the apparatus, and although we both remembered the words well, so that I could prompt her if she hesitated, the lament recorded was a mere shadow of the first. A second repetition was even less successful.[73]

The significance of the lament as a musical genre in Hungarian folk music consists in its being the only example of prose recitative, and almost the only example of improvisation. It is incorrect to call children's songs and 'regös' songs recitative. *Recitativo* means singing without beat or measurable rhythm; it is musical prose on the borders of music and speech, and its 'music' is only a variation in pitch. It has no rhythm except speech rhythm, and there are no clearly defined bars or regularly repeated rhythmical formulae. In children's songs, however, this is not the case, and there is also bodily movement to regulate the rhythmic pulse; they provide the purest example of music with an exact beat.

The lament, on the contrary, is pure recitative. It has a rhythm that cannot be measured in bars, the sections between pauses are unequal, and the repetition of melodic phrases is irregular and cannot be divided into bars. Yet the examples show that the idea of some definite melody hovers above the freely flowing prose. The lament consists usually of the irregular repetition of two tune-lines. If the starting note is taken as an octave (8), the first line finishes on 5, the second on 4. (But transposed according to the final note, the cadences are 2 and 1.) All the line-endings on 5 and 4 are repeated *ad libitum* according to the length of what has to be said.

The first example represents this type of two lines. The original final is given at the beginning:

117

Di-csér-tes-sék a Jé-zus Krisz-tus! ad- jon Is-ten szë-rën-csés jó-j-es-tét, i-dës pá-rocs-kám! Né-künk szë-ren-csé-set né-këd üd-vös-sí-gës- set.

(II) Jaj de nëm hit-tem vó-na pá-rom, hogy oly-lyan ha-mar el-ma-rad-junk ëgy-más-tó! Jaj még tëg-nap ily-lyen-kor is csak úgy biz-tat-tá ën- gë-met:

(III) Në fíj asz-szon, nëm ha-lok mëg, nëm ha-gyó-lak még ti- gëd!

Jaj pá-rocs-kám mé' hat-tá itt, eb-be ja szo-mo-ró vi-lág- ba. *etc.*

In rare cases, the two tune-lines are augmented by two shorter ones, one
ending on ♭3, the other on 1:

Zsére (Nyitra County), 1915. **K.**

118

(The text is unknown) Min-dën ëgy-gye vi-gann es-kü-dött, fe-hér ru- há-, ba, fe-hér ko-szo-ró-ba, pi-ros pár- tá-ba, de bi-zony én fe-ke- të ru- há- ba, ződ pár- tá- ba, ződ ko-szo- ró-ba, még csak ak-kor

së vót ne-këm víg ked-vem ëggy ó- ra hosz-szát së, nëm tok én sëm-mi víg ked-vet mő- te í- lëk e vi- lá- gon! Jaj í- dës jó pá- rocs-kám, í- dës párt- fo-gócs-kám. A- lig bír-tam ve-led ki-húz-nyi két esz-ten-dőt, a-lig bír-tam ve-led ki-húz-nyi két esz-ten-dőt mind öz-vegy-sig-rë ma-rad-tam.

etc.

This form also uses the whole octave. If it comes down to 1, it does not begin again at the upper octave but, as seen in the continuation marked II, it climbs up, normally to the seventh, so that the upper octave may never be heard again. The irregularity of the repetitions is also well illustrated in this example. In its first section, the line-ending on the fourth is repeated seven times; the fifth appears once. In the second section, the fifth is omitted, and three line-endings on the fourth succeed each other.

Since the shorter tune reappears in the longer as its upper section, two explanations are possible:

1. The two-line form may be assumed to be a truncated variation, a fragment of the longer one. This is supported by the fact that a type is known in which the first line-ending is missing, making it a three-line song with endings 4, ♭3 and 1:

Csitár (Nyitra County), 1914. K.

Original final

Lyányom, lyányom, kedves ga-lam-bom, I-lon-kám, Már të csak a-zo-ka-tə mind vég-höz vit-ted azt a nagy ke-se-rű- sí- gët, a-kit né-këm o-koz-tál.

etc.

Laments of this structure appear sporadically in other areas as well.

2. The two-line song is the original form, and the larger forms grew out of its various supplementations. This is borne out by the fact that the two-

line form of narrow range is the only type of lament that is widespread through-out the entire language area, and is to be found side by side with various local forms.

The new volume of laments (CMPH Vol. V, 1966), has brought to light a surprising wealth of new material. When, after the completion of the first four volumes of the *Corpus*, work began on the complementary collection of laments, we were surprised to find so many still alive. A glance at the data for numbers collected and period of collection reveals this unexpected richness:

Up to 1918: 37 laments,   5 parodies
1919–1951: 48 laments,   9 parodies
1952–1963: 503 laments, 183 parodies

To a large extent, the development of tape recording is to be credited with this success, but not exclusively so. Our people too have changed during half a century. They are no more timid and distrustful; they have become aware of their own value and of the value of their traditions; and it is against this background of understanding that people now view and assist the work aimed at revealing their traditions, though they too understand that these traditions must pass away.

This immense body of new material (which, with the exception of a narrow—Northwestern Transdanubian—region originates from the whole territory of the Hungarian language) contains a great wealth of new and un-familiar types. These vary from region to region, and this was the reason why the geographical principle was chosen as the basis of the system of types adopted in the volume. The types of lament from individual regions differ in their line-endings and tonal range, but a *recitativo* descending melodic line, and improvisation, are common to them; only the line cadences—the pauses—offer some kind of regularity, in a great diversity of types.

There is also a regional difference in the role of diatonic and pentatonic structure. By and large the lament, particularly in its short form, is diatonic; but there are examples (or types) everywhere in which, to a greater or lesser extent, pentatonic structure or pentatonic turns emerge either in the lower or the upper section. Indeed, there are types (especially in areas populated by Székely and Csángó) that are clearly pentatonic in their entirety. All this is obviously connected with the folksong style prevailing in a given territory.[74]

One type of Transdanubian lament shows the same pentatonic transfor-mation as other five-note tunes of that region (see p. 25).

Nagybajom (Somogy County), 1922. K.

120

J-Jaj, ə né-ném-asz-szony, né-ném-asz-szony!   áld-jo mëg a jó *i*Is- ten,

kend-nek min-dën ë' sszëm po-rát   a ho-vá j-ëgy szëm el- e- sik.

i Jaj! mér ollyan i-gaz vót kê hoz-zánk,   əm-mér vot kê oly-lyan ı-gaz

ta-lán még a szü-lés   fáj-dol-mát is əm-mëg-osz-tot-ta kêd az é-dös-a-

nyánk-kol   *i* Jaj szı-vem-nek fe-le, szı-vem-nek fe-le, ked-ves jó né-

Slower

ném-asz-szony,   ki az én é-dës-a-nyámnok se-gét kê ne-vê-nyi ben-nün- ket.
etc.

CMPH Vol. V, No. 91. Tápé (Csongrád County).

Parlando ♪ = 132 -126

121

5)   (2

... Mért is hagyott kend ijen ár - ván,   é - dö - sə jó a -   nyám,

fe-lejt-he-tet-len   jó   anyám?   m- Mért is hagyott i-jen á - rə-ván?

Së ó-dös- a-pám most mán, së jédös- a -   nyám,   kedves jó   anyám!

Mit i - zen-jek   annak a kedə-ves jó   é - dös- a-pám - nak,

fe-lejt - hetetlen jó   a - pám-nak?
etc.

90

On the Great Hungarian Plain, cadences on 2 are more frequent (or as frequent) as those on ♭3 in the large form. It would appear that the 5, 4, 2, 1 line-endings of Ex. No. 121 shown, are transpositions to the fourth below of the 5, 4 cadences of the small form.

It seems then that the rather frequent 4, 1 cadential structure has also preserved a fourth relationship in a single line-ending:

CMPH Vol. V, No. 125. Lónya (Bereg County).

Sometimes the order of the cadences is reversed, the lower comes first, and the upper closes the larger units:

CMPH Vol. V, No. 58. Gamás (Somogy County).

(This order—in the case of a melody in the minor—gives a feeling of the Phrygian scale. Even without it, Phrygian character may emerge in our laments, for example, in Southern Transdanubia.)

The structure of diatonic laments with 5, 4, 2, 1 line-endings may become re-interpreted in explicitly pentatonic forms—among the Székely—as *re-do-la-so*, which in Hungarian songs, according to the customary $g = la$ transposition, corresponds to 4, ♭3, 1, VII:

CMPH Vol. V, No. 160. Gyimesközéplok (Csík County).

124

Jaj lelkëm, lelkëm, jó társom,   nëgyvennégybe elesëtt, mëgölte az az   át-kozott háború-ú!

Jaj,   András, András,   hol van a te sí-ro -   od?

Jaj hol van a te gyászos sirod?   Sose tudom még a kërësztfádot se fël-keres-ni.

Similarly the formula of the small form becomes 1, VII instead of 2, 1.

CMPH Vol. V, No. 150. Mákófalva (Kolozs County). (From Székely resettled in Karcag-Berekfürdőtelep, Jász-Nagykun-Szolnok County.)

125

Most az u-tol-só   búcsú-nál   vagyunk,

most már itt këll hagynunk,   mert már csak a   sír-hal-mo-dat   lát-juk.

Isten veled,   drága kis lëjányom,   a-lugyál csëndesen, az ö-rök nyúgalomba!

However, the major character of the diatonic hexachord may persist even in pentatonic form, that is, its lowest note will continue to be felt as *do*, and not as *so*; at such times the lament moves in pentatony to end on *do*.

126

Parlando ♩ = cca 75

A-pu-ka, édĕs a-pu-kám, mér hattál el i-jen ár - ván?

Mer én azt nem gondoltam, hogy elhagysz tĕ ár - ván,

ebbe ja szomoru-ság - ba, ebbe a nagy bá - nat - ba!

In Ex. No. 76 we find another, rare type of song with recitation on *do-re-mi*. This is akin to the psalm-type of melody quoted on pp. 56–57. This type appears only in laments among the Csángó in one or two places, where also the last specimens of the recitation-type of tune may still be heard.

The fact that a connection exists between local song-types and local forms of laments was pointed out in the case of the Székely people by Bálint Sárosi.[75] The Székely sing so-called 'complaints' that represent a transitional form between the local pentatonic lament and local pentatonic strophic melodies. Their melodic turns and construction are identical, and they are also strophic, but with a variable number of syllables to the line. It is as though this showed the road of development from improvised lament to strictly organized stanzas with a fixed number of syllables.

In Nagyszalonta (Bihar County), and in its vicinity, in Bihar and Hajdú Counties as well as in several places in central Transylvania, it is no longer possible to hear improvised personal laments in prose; instead, rhymed texts are sung to a fixed tune. Although traces of church burial-chants are to be heard in these verses, the textual content is generally independent still. This is apparently a later stage of development, when the individual's personal expression of grief gives way to a typical fixed text.

Yet this too is most certainly a lament, because the nearest female relative of the deceased sings it beside the corpse in the cemetery. As late as 1916, it was customary for mourners to scatter in the cemetery after the burial ceremony, each at the headstone of his own dead, and there to continue the lament, so that the entire cemetery resounded with weeping and wailing. In the course of more recent collecting this was experienced in other regions as well. A few surviving parodies show that improvised individual laments used to be customary in this village, also.[76]

In other places, laments were not always linked with burial. In Ghymes (Nyitra County), many years ago, I watched an old woman alone in a cemetery, walking every Sunday afternoon round the headstone of her son's grave, sobbing quietly as she recited to the tune of the lament. She stopped as I approached. Several times during the First World War, I observed that solitary women, for years without news of sons or husbands would lament alone at home for hours on a winter evening, while they sat spinning: 'Alas, dear John, dear son, what a sad life I lead! Alas, without son or husband, I am quite forsaken and alone. I have nobody to speak to. Alas for you, dear child, suffering in a foreign country. I have no news of you, and your father lies wounded in hospital, wounded on the battlefield...' Our volume quotes recent examples of this practice (see CMPH Vol. V, p. 46).

Mourning ceremonies must not be confused with the vigil (or wake), when several elderly women keep vigil the whole night long beside a laid-out corpse, singing songs for the dead and praying.[77] These used to receive some present from the relatives of the deceased, as well as food and drink, and this may have given rise to the legend of paid mourning women.

In some ways, the funeral song of the village cantor has taken over the function of the mourning song. He would 'compose' it himself, and intone it, in most cases, to the tune of some well-known church chant. In it, the dead man calls by name on the relatives he has left behind, taking his leave of them one by one. This might be an old custom, but has not yet been systematically investigated. It, too, is a sign of emergence from old folk-culture: people pay experts, 'specialists,' to do what in older times each would have done for himself.

94

VI INTERRELATIONS IN FOLK MUSIC

What have Hungarians given to their neighbours, and what have they been given in return? Béla Bartók's study,[78] with 127 tunes as examples, offers convincing proof that our neighbours have not materially influenced the formation of Hungarian melodic style, either now or in the past, but have all tended to fall under its influence to a greater or lesser extent. That is why certain ancient Hungarian tunes with original Eastern characteristics occasionally appear in Slovak, Croatian or Rumanian collections. It is the more recent folksongs, however, which have very considerably extended the field of influence of Hungarian music, far beyond its linguistic frontiers. Traces of these are found from Moravia to Moldavia (Rumania), and from the region of the River Mur to Galicia.

As far as foreign influences on Hungarian music are concerned, Bartók ascribed a greater role to transmission by cultured or semicultured classes than to direct transfer from peasantry to peasantry. This is natural in view of the considerations previously advanced (Chapter I). The middle classes of foreign stock brought with them songs of their former homeland, and the second generation, growing up as Hungarians, began to sing them in Hungarian. This explains how the international, Eastern-European, folksong material, mentioned by Bartók and so far inadequately defined, came into being.[79] This material is to be found among every East-Central European people, and consists of a number of 'migrating' tunes, the origins of which it would be difficult (perhaps impossible) to establish. It may be that more detailed sociological information than that at present available will throw light on this.

The Hungarian folk-tradition shows marked resistance to German tunes. The chief reason for this is that the German language has systems of stress and rhythm alien to Hungarian. Since the eighteenth century, the cultured class has taken over many German tunes and created similar ones in the same spirit. (These are the songs that K. Szini called 'folksongs of the nobility' in the mid-nineteenth century, and of which János Arany wrote,[80] 'the text is florid, the melody German.') Scarcely any of these have been taken over by peasants, and iambic tunes were notably ignored; if peasant singers adopted them, they put the accent on the short syllable of the iamb.

a) Istensegíts (Bukovina), 1914. K.
b) Kide (Kolozs County). P. Járdányi.

127 a

Jó es- tét bar- na lány. Mi lö- le té- ge- det?

b

Vi- rá- gim, vi- rá- gim, Gyö- nyö- rű vi- rá- gim.

Ta- lán a va- cso- rád Nem i- gen jól e- sett.

Főd- re bo- ru- ja tok, En- gem si- ras- sa- tok.

The upper tune is the version believed to be closer to the unknown original (Bukovina: 1914, Z. Kodály). Below it is the 'Magyarized' version from P. Járdányi's monograph *A kidei magyarság világi zenéje* (The Secular Music of Hungarians of Kide; Kolozsvár, 1943).

They found it easier to accept rhythms with a stressed beginning:

Doboz (Békés County), 1906. B.

128

Hogy ve- ti el a pa- raszt Las- san- kint a za- bot?

Így ve- ti el a pa- raszt Las- san- kint a za- bot.

var.:

(For a German variant see Böhme: *Deutsches Kinderlied*, p. 497.)[81]

The melody of the song 'Megcsalt férj' (The deceived husband) is also German:[82]

The 79-year-old folk singer, István Beke, from Gicce (Gömör County, 1913). (See his song on p. 103)

The hurdy-gurdy player, István Balla, from Szentes

Shepherd playing the pipe. Fadd, Tolna County

É - des ked-ves   fe - le - sé-gem!   Mi baj an-gya - lom?

Mit ke - res itt   a nyer-ges ló   az   ud - va - ro-mon?

As yet it is impossible to say which songs came directly from German settlers in Hungary, and which through the Hungarian middle classes. The role of church hymns will be discussed in a later chapter.

It is comparatively easy to distinguish German from Hungarian tunes; in most cases they have retained a special function—as, for instance, the German students' song 'Ballag már a vén diák' (The old student has started to wander), 'Es ritten drei Reiter zum Tore hinaus, ade!' (See, for example, K. Neumann–H. Dombrowski: *Der Spielmann*, 1930, p. 66.) At one time this was the favourite farewell song of graduates from high school, and in the Vác district it is still sung by folk singers to the text of a Hungarian ballad. Only rarely does a German tune merge with a Hungarian one; for example, 'Ha nékem szóltál volna' (If only you had told me).[83]

Direct folk-contact was closest between Hungarians and Slovaks. Slovak glaziers and itinerant tinkers were always wandering about the Hungarian countryside, but it was principally as harvesters that Slovaks crowded down to the Hungarian Plain. In years of plenty, a Zobor farmer with half a dozen acres would never harvest without at least one or two Slovak harvesters. Hungarian peasants would learn Slovak songs with Slovak texts, even if they did not understand a word. Other songs would gain Hungarian words:

Felsőireg (Tolna County), 1907. B.

Parlando

— Hol   jár- tál   Ru- zsics- kám   i- lyen   ko- rán,
Hogy   i- lyen   har- ma- tos   a   ro- ko- lyád?

— Zöld   er- dő-   ben   jár- tam,   É- des   ró- zsám.
zöld   fü- vet   a- rat- tam,

A distorted form of the original Slovak text was sung as the second stanza. The Hungarian text above is a translation of it.

Even greater numbers of songs were learnt by Slovak workers from Hungarians. Any Slovak folksong collection, glanced through at random, abounds with them, and includes several examples of the more recent popular art-songs.

But in Hungary these 'guest songs' never lost their foreign quality. 'Adoption' begins when the foreign tune acquires Hungarian words. It is then sung by Hungarians as a Hungarian tune; they are no longer conscious of its foreignness and feel it to be one of theirs. There are not many of these, however.[84]

This is the simplest kind of loan-influence, and the easiest to demonstrate. Complications arise when the complete tune is no longer recognizable, and half (or less) has been left, with new melodic shapes to fill the gaps; or when just a few lines, rhythmic formulae or melodic constructions have been taken over. In this field much research has still to be done.

Information recently disclosed about the Mari has opened up a possible new line of approach to the 'Kolomejka' form. Up to now, we believed with Bartók, that the Hungarian type of 'swineherd's song' (see Chapter II) originated in the Ruthenian* 'Kolomejka' form.[85] (See the Swineherd's Song from Karád on p. 29, Ex. No. 14.)

In the Mari material there are many examples both of the shorter (Ruthenian) and of the longer (Hungarian) forms. (For Mari examples of the shorter form see Exs. Nos. 36 and 41–42; for the longer, Exs. Nos. 5 and 6.) The Mari line-endings almost always have three syllables, ♩‿♩ ♩, which is also fairly common in the Hungarian endings, so that the two-syllable line-ending should not be considered obligatory. (It also occasionally appears in the Mari.)

The Ruthenian examples always have the line-ending ♩ ♩, or ♩ ♪ ♪. Thus a characteristic rhythmical peculiarity, common to Hungarian and Mari examples, is entirely absent from Ruthenian examples. Even more significant is the fact that all the Mari and most of the Hungarian examples are pentatonic and repeat the first section at the lower fifth. Another typical common characteristic is liberty in the number of syllables to the line. (For example, in Ex. No. 14 on p. 29,4/3/4/2 alternates with 4/4/4/2.)

Neither of these peculiarities exists in the Ruthenian material.[86] If we compare examples 64a b (Ex. No. 131) in Bartók: *Népzenénk* (Our Folk Music...), it is impossible to believe that the Ruthenian is the original and the Hungarian the copy. It is far more probable that the Hungarian is the original: it has greater vitality, a sharper outline, a pure fifth construction, as well as being purely pentatonic, with only one unaccented *pien* note. Our example, No. 10, does not even have this extraneous note. In the Ruthenian tune neither fifth construction nor the pentatonic system are present any longer. It is, so

---

* Ruthenia = Sub-Carpathian Russia (Carpatho-Ukraine). (Translator's note.)

a) Barslédec (Bars County), 1907. K.
b) Dolha (Máramaros County), 1911. B.

131 a

Tempo giusto

Lá-nyok ül- nek a to-rony- ba a- rany- ko - szo - ru- ban.

b

♩ = 72

Ta ne sa-ma'm, ta ne sa-ma'm, Ka-li- nu la - ma- la

Ar- ra men- nek a le- gé- nyek sar- kan- tyus csiz- má- ban.

La - mal e - i mij mi- lenj- kjij, [Ja- liš pri- gi- na- la.]

to speak, a faded, threadbare copy of the Hungarian, and also lacks the larger, four-line form that is so important both in Mari and Hungarian material. The fifth construction also occurs in some of the instrumental dance pieces based on this larger form (e.g. No. 72 in Bartók: *Népzenénk*). It may be that they, too, conceal an ancient Eastern heritage. To solve the problem, more detailed exploration of the whole of Eastern European instrumental and vocal music is needed, not to mention research into possible Ruthenian–Mari contacts. Naturally, this does not exclude the possibility that other tunes, with 8, 6, 8, 6, syllables and without fifth construction, are Ruthenian in origin.

One further point that must be mentioned is that since the fifteenth century Hungarian literature has used the verse form of the 'Kolomejka' (fourteen syllables, 4/4/4/2, and fifteen syllables, 4/4/4/3). It is being examined by Hungarian scholars for traces of medieval Latin influence.[87]

CHURCH MUSIC: GREGORIAN CHANT

As the first important cultural influence on Western Europe, Christianity brought with it the great international treasury of Gregorian chant. Its influence on Hungarian folk music, such as it was, was not that of an abstract tonal system, but that of living music. Peasants could only accept tunes, not ecclesiastical modes. These latter were only abstracted from living music at a later date, and even then not without considerable arbitrariness. In the extraordinarily complex question of Gregorian influence, basic research is still entirely lacking, and all that can be done is to offer a few facts.

The relationship of a few Hungarian tunes to Gregorian psalmody has already been indicated. It is an open question whether the Magyars came into contact with that part of Gregorian chant which was Eastern in origin—and hence also with Gregorian psalmody—*before* they were converted to Christianity. * This might be established by research into the remarkable spread of the psalmodic type among related peoples, as has already been mentioned (see Chapter II). Since other Gregorian elements have also been adopted by peasants, all that can be deduced for the moment is that there must have been very frequent opportunities of hearing the models.

Thus a Passiontide *Alleluia* is recognizable in this 'harvest-home' song from the Zobor region.[88]

a) CMPH Vol. II. No. 309. Pográny (Nyitra County), 1906. K.

Tempo giusto

132 a

El- vé- gez-tük, el- vé- gez-tük az a- ra-tást, az a- ra-tást.
Ké-szijj gaz-da, ké-szíjj gaz-da jó ál- do-mást, jó ál- do-mást.

b

Al- le- lu- ia, al- le-lu-ia, al-le- lu- ia,

* Hungary was converted to Christianity about A.D. 1000. (Translator's note.)

Careful search would very probably bring other such borrowings to light. It is for more detailed research to decide whether they reached the Hungarian song-repertory directly through liturgical chant with Latin texts, through Hungarian graduals, or through contact with neighbouring peoples.

FOLK HYMNS

It would be well worthwhile making a study of the connections between Hungarian hymns and folksong, even if only from a textual point of view. For centuries this was practically the only literary verse-influence to reach the villages. The secular lyric may well have been adopted through oral tradition; but where church music was concerned, there were printed books with fixed texts. Although people for the most part learnt hymns by heart, the texts were always at hand and it was not so easy to change them. This meant that the formation of variants was confined to the tunes. Only after 1607 (A. Molnár: *Psalterium*) or 1651 *(Cantus Catholici)* did Hungarian hymnbooks begin to be supplied with tunes.[89] Nevertheless, certain flourishing folk tunes today show forms completely changed from the printed versions in various psalm-books. A collection of folk variants would provide much valuable data towards understanding the basic laws governing variant-formation.

'Secular' and 'sacred' song, that is, *nóta* and *ének*, co-exist in the folk mind as they do in the majority of old Hungarian verse anthologies in manuscript. For the cultured classes, church music was confined to church, but for the peasants it had a part to play in life outside the church. How often could pious old women be heard singing hymns for hours at a time in farm courtyards on Sunday afternoons, or on winter evenings in the house! In some parts of the country, hymns would even be sung while working in the fields.

And not only in Hungary: everywhere hymns have been inextricably interwoven with secular songs, and their tunes are often secular in origin. As early as the twelfth century, French secular songs were given sacred versions,[90] and at the time of the Reformation sacred texts were often set to secular tunes. The problem of origin is frequently insoluble.

In Hungary, a few tunes still have both sacred and secular texts, side by side. Presumably because of great differences in tempo and rhythm, the peasants are not aware that the tunes are identical, even when the same person sings both forms. The following groups, for example, are variants of the same tune.

1. The tune of the well-known hymn 'Üdvözlégy, Krisztusnak drága szent teste (Hail, dear, holy body of Christ), known as early as the seventeenth century, is the same as that of many secular songs. For instance:

a drinking song from Nagyszalonta.[91]

Rubato ♩ = 112–116

133

Éj! mën- jünk el in- nen   mert   itt mëg- ver- nek!

(Accelerated . . . . 1) . . .)

Ne mën- jünk ad- dig el,   míg   he- ge- dül- nek.

(♩ = 88–104)

Hozz bort a   ma- gyar- nak,   pá- jin- kát a   tót- nak,

(♩ = 92)

Sërt   a   ní- mët-   nek!

or: 1) dig el,

a comic song in eighteenth-century manuscripts.[92]

Ádám Pálóczi-Horváth, No. 265.

134

Á - rok- szál - lá   sá   nál   volt egy   ve- sze- de - lem,
Mely- nek   o   ka   va   la   ko- pasz   fe- je   de - lem.

Haj- tott, haj- tott, haj- rá   haj- tott,   Nem vólt en- ge- de- lem.
mint a   sár- kány, úgy or   dí- tott,

a fragment in ballad style from the Zobor region.[93]

Lédec (Bars County), 1907. K.

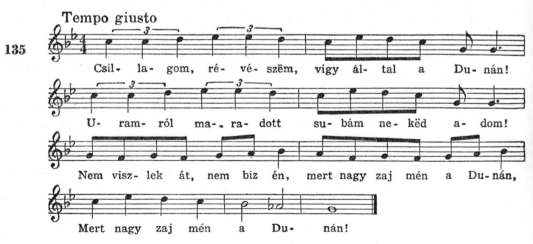

Tempo giusto

135

Csil- la- gom, ré- vé- szëm, vigy ál- tal a   Du- nán!

U- ram- ról ma- ra- dott   su- bám ne- këd   a- dom!

Nem visz- lek át, nem biz én,   mert nagy zaj mén   a   Du- nán,

Mert nagy   zaj   mén   a   Du-   nán!

What is more, the entire group is related to a tune-type of the so-called 'Rákóczi-nóta,' of which the following is a late descendant. It was sung by seventy-nine-year-old István Beke.[94]

Gicce (Gömör County), 1913, K.

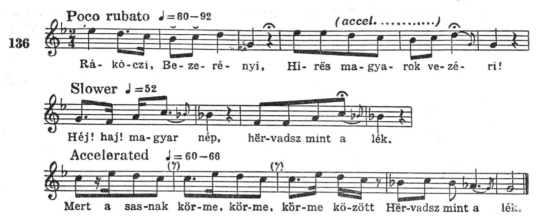

It is interesting that this tune has had a double function ever since its first appearance. In the *Kájoni MS.* (1634–1671)[95] it is found as a dance piece with the title of 'Chorea' and in Náray's *Lyra coelestis* (1695) as a hymn (Exs. Nos. 137, 138).

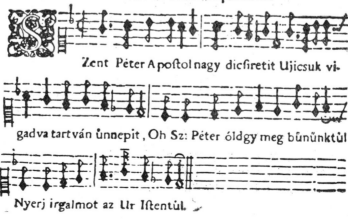

2. In his *Hungarian Folk Music*, Bartók conditionally assigned the first example to the style because of its AABB tune construction, though it is not in fact typically pentatonic. It is also sung as a hymn.[96]

3. A Church hymn known as early as 1674 has the same tune as the folk-ballad ´Julis Benke.´[97] This is the more remarkable because variants with both sacred and secular texts are widespread (all in the region of Csík). There is still no evidence that peasants realize that the tunes are the same.

Tekerőpatak (Csík County), 1906. B.

4. This is another harvesting song from the Zobor region. It too, has many different sacred texts, and appears in late eighteenth-century manuscripts as a funeral hymn.[98]

In 1855 the Zsasskovszky brothers used this tune as the setting of St. Stephen's Hymn, one of Hungary's best-loved historical hymns, beginning 'Ah, hol vagy, magyarok' (Where art thou, guiding star of Hungary). The text first appeared in 1797 (in Bozóky's *Book of Songs*) but can be found even

104

before this in manuscript form, without a musical setting; there is no evidence that it was sung before 1855. The tune itself is of German origin (Zahn: *Die Melodien der deutschen evangelischen Kirchenlieder*, No. 5257, from 1686):

142

5. The well-known Hungarian song 'Nem ettem én ma egyebet' (I have eaten nothing else today) is a variant of the 134th Geneva psalm, with almost identically the same rhythms as the original. Nothing is known about how this happened.[99] Since psalms were never metrically sung in Hungary, a rhythmic variant could never have been formed from its living form. A musically cultivated person must have fitted the tune to the text which then spread as a 'secular counterpart.'

6. The peregrinations of the following tune are not easy to trace. Jacopone da Todi's hymn 'Cur mundus militat' must have been one of the most popular in Hungary.[100] Since the time of Péter Bornemissza's Song-Book (1582)[101] it has been printed innumerable times in Hungarian hymnbooks, with the text 'Mit bízik a világ' (Why does he whose fortune...). It has three tunes. In the first two lines of one of them (Ex. No. 143a)[102] we recognize the tune of the folk-ballad 'Bíró Szép Anna' (The Beautiful Anna Bíró) (b).[103] It is a tune of foreign origin: Bäumker derives it from a German source of 1625.[104] That the first half of this tune has engraved itself so deeply in folk conssciousness is perhaps due to yet another tune, which only appears in one Transylvanian hymnbook[105] with the text 'Mit bízik a világ' and is popular even today as the setting of a funeral hymn 'Harc ember élete' (Man's life is a struggle). Although its second half is quite different, the first two lines are quite close to a). It is quoted (c) with the erroneous text to be found in the *Kolozsvár Song-Book* The flats in brackets are confirmed by the better editions.

Finally, the peasantry must often have heard the beginning of this tune in the form of the dirge 'Jaj, melly hamar múlik e világ öröme' (Alas, how quickly the joy of this world passes!). The tune of this consists of the first two lines of 'Cur mundus' or 'Harc ember élete' with the addition of a six-syllable concluding line (d).[106] Peasants thus knew the tune in a shortened form as well, and this must have been the immediate reason for its adoption.

143 a — Mit bízik e Vi-lág   ő ál-nok-ságában   Ki-nek ſze-ren-csé-je vagyonelromláſban.

b — Igy iszik,úgy iszik,   három hajdu legény hñ Bi-ró Zsigmondnénak kötött kapujába.

sic

c — *CurMundus militat ſub va-na glori-a   Cujus proſperitas   eſt tranſitori-a.*

d — Jaj mely hamar múlik a' Vi-lág ö-rö-me   Hir-te-len vál-to-zik minden ékessége.

7. The preface to Albert Molnár Szenczi's *Psalms,* 1607, reads: '...I see that a large part of the Psaltery has been translated and set by distinguished men to Czech, German and Hungarian tunes.' The spread of Czech tunes in Hungary is proved by the fact that several of them even penetrated the repertory of secular folksong. The two examples below (Exs. Nos. 144a and 146a) are from a Czech hymnbook of 1576.[107] The first of the Hungarian counterparts is well known throughout Hungary (Ex. No. 144b); the variant in Bartók's *Hungarian Folk Music,* No. 259b (Ex. No. 145) agrees with the Czech original in a few notes even more closely than the example given here:

Ghymes (Nyitra County). K

144 a

b — Szöl- lő   hë-gyin   ëgy kör- te- fa   tö-vinn áll,   tö-vinn áll.

Ëgy-gyik á- gán   Rë- ci- ka Të- réz   csak úgy   sír- do- gál.

Tempo giusto ♩ = 92

145

Szé- pen szól a kis pa- csir- ta Fönn a ma- gas- ba,

El köll men- nem ka- to- ná- nak. Lá- nyok si- rat- nak.

The other Hungarian counterpart is less well known:

b) Andrásfalva (Bukovina)[108], 1914. K.

146 a

b

Ré- gën vót, so- ká lesz, Míg o- lyan ró- zsám lesz,

Ki- nek gyën- ge kar- ja Két vál- lam ta- 'kar- ja.

There is no doubt that these two Hungarian tunes are of Czech origin. The divergence in the third line is not so great as that to be found in related groups of variants. The descending sixth has disappeared here, too (see p. 74).[109]

8. The following tune, preserved in a thirteenth-century Spanish manuscript, probably came to Hungary by way of the Czechs.[110] The Hungarian version used to be sung in the spinning rooms of the Zobor region, late at night, so that the spinners could keep each other awake. The second verse of the song refers to the courting couples present.

147

Ben po de San- ta Ma- ri- a Guarir de to- da po- çon

Në a- lugy el két szë- mëm-nek vë- lá- ga,

Pois mad- re do que trill- lou O ba- si- lis- que o dra- gon.

Majd fĕl- kél már pi- ros haj- nal csil- lag- ja.

The comparison may seem a trifle bold, but it is certain that the tune-type is identical, even if the Hungarian is shorter. For a thousand years, Hungary has been linked with the migrations of European tunes; when more is known about medieval music, the exploration of which is only just beginning, it will be clear that late descendants also of medieval tune-types have survived in Hungarian folksong.

It is not as if one or two tune-lines or motifs have been wrenched from their contexts and set against each other. They are complete tune-constructions. A certain amount of resemblance could be a coincidence, but the correspondence of organic wholes and essential tune-structures can hardly be explained without assuming a common origin.

This is not the place, however, to discuss the implications of a few scattered traces. An immense field of research is still awaiting investigation; but even from the data already provided, it is clear that numerous contacts existed between hymns and the folk-tradition, and it was probably through this contact that certain Western-European tune-types reached Hungary.

To conclude, here is yet another pair of tunes in which the folk tune (well known in the Zobor region) appears as an enlarged edition of the hymn tune. The folk tune is recorded in the major key in a seventeenth-century Hungarian manuscript,[111] but village folk sing a minor variant.[112]

148 a

Di- csér- jük Jé- zus szent- sé- ges szűz Any- ját

Tempo giusto ♩=112

b

Ez a kis lány ak- kor sír, mi- kor ko- szo- rú van a fe- jén.

A szép menny- or- szág szin- a- rany- ját,

Megy az Is- ten há- zá- ba, rá- gon- dol a lá- nyok so- rá- ra.

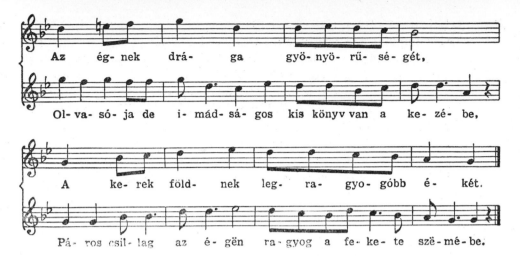

Az ég- nek drá- ga gyö- nyö- rű- sé- gét,

Ol- va- só- ja de i- mád- sá- gos kis könyv van a ke- zé- be,

A ke- rek föld- nek leg- ra- gyo- góbb é- két.

Pá- ros csil- lag az é- gën ra- gyog a fe- ke- te szë- mé- be.

Even this essentially Hungarian song, a favourite with village girls, is connected by hidden threads with the West. In support of this statement let us quote—like the French *chanson* on p. 63 (Ex. No. 79)—the beginning of a sixteenth-century 'Ricercare' for viola (from Ganassi's *Regola Rubertina*, 1542).[113]

149  etc.

SECULAR ART-MUSIC

The folk repertory has always grown by borrowing from art-music. Previously, when the social and cultural differences between one man and the next were less marked than they are now, this borrowing took place more easily. In the book of the humanist Marzio Galeotto *Concerning the wise and witty words and deeds of King Matthias*[114] *(De egregie, sapienter, iocose dictis ac factis regis Mathiae ad ducem Johannem eius filium liber)* the author comments with surprise that *c.* 1480 the nobles and people of Hungary had the same language and 'they equally understand the songs written in the Hungarian language.' It is obvious from this that they heard each other's songs.

It must constantly be remembered that in those days knowledge of music was diffused entirely through oral tradition. Up to the nineteenth century, musical notation only meant incomprehensible and superfluous hieroglyphics to folk singers. In the sixteenth century, the text may have meant little more, for Hungarian bibliographers have no knowledge of printed secular songs of that time; even the love poems of Bálint Balassa, the greatest Hungarian lyric poet of the sixteenth century, were left in manuscript. Fragments of this unpublished poetry were preserved in living song, so that present-day folk variants can be based on manuscripts two or three hundred years old. From time to time during the eighteenth and nineteenth centuries, these variants were printed in pamphlet form, by which time printing was helping to preserve the texts as well. Nevertheless, folk-tradition was (and is) the only real preserver of these tunes.

About 1906, old peasant women in remote villages of the Zobor region still knew the fragment quoted below. The complete text has been preserved in the seventeenth-century *Vásárhelyi daloskönyv* (Vásárhelyi Song-Book).[115]

Kolon (Nyitra County), 1906. K.

The original nine-line verse of Balassa (3×6.6.7) has been reduced to six lines, but there is nothing missing from the tune, which is completed by the repetition of the first half. The text is sixteenth century and may be by Balassa or one of his contemporaries; the tune too may be from the same period. There is nothing that argues against this supposition, which is supported by resemblance to the 'Cronica' tune of András Farkas, published in 1538 :[116]

István Dobai's 'Siralmas volt nékem' (Sad it was for me) was first published by K. Thaly from the seventeenth century *Szencsei MS.*[117] Two of its verses and its splendid tune were known to old women about 1900.[118] It is worth comparing with a variant in the manuscript *Song-Book* of Ádám Pálóczi-Horváth, 1813. In form it agrees with a variant found in other manuscripts, less than half a century older.[119] Naturally, Ádám Pálóczi-Horváth's manuscript could not have helped the spread of the tune, still less the other manuscripts mentioned, which all gave it other texts.

b) Siklód (Udvarhely County). V.

This parallel shows that even if there were many written examples of old tunes in existence, it would still not be possible to gain a complete notion of what they were in performance. Old music manuscripts merely give a skeleton of the tune; key and rhythm are often indeterminate. This skeleton can only be changed to living flesh and blood through living, traditional performance. A complete and faithful reconstruction can only be given for tunes that have been preserved in the living tradition as well.[120]

Though the spread of lyric poetry took place through oral tradition, it is known that the sixteenth and seventeenth-century 'historical songs' (news songs, rhyming chronicles, versified short stories) were also spread by printing. Nevertheless it is memory that chiefly helps to keep them alive. About 1910 it was not unusual for an old man to know by heart the greater part of the *History of István Kádár* (first edition 1657); it was more than probable that he had never read it, and perhaps that he could not even read.

153

Szër- nyű nagy rom- lás- ra ké- szül Pan- no- ni- a,

Ki- nek mint tën- gër- nek meg- á- ra- dó hob- ja.

Sok bú- nak, bá- nat- nak kör- nyül- vët- te ár- ja,

Mert a vi- té- zëk- nek e- sëtt ma ëgy héj- ja.

I was surprised one day to hear a few verses of the *History of Argirus* (a sixteenth-century poem) from a peasant singer. I made a thorough search but could find no copy in the area, though many people remembered seeing it in a printed *Historia*.[121]

154

Ka- to- na va- gyok én, or- szág ő- re- ző- je,

Sír az él- dës- a- nyám, hogy el- visz- nek tő- le,

Sír az él- dës- a- nyám, a ró- zsám mëg gyá- szol,

Fe- ke- te gyász- vi- rág bú- sul ab- la- ká- ba.

The singer of the following fragment, János Király Vicenc, sixty-year-old farmer from Nagypeszek (Hont County), could only tell me that his grandmother, born at Tök (Pest County), had learnt it from the village miller. He had no idea that it was a verse from a work by János Bodó Szentmártoni, *Az tékozló fiúnak históriái* (Stories of the Prodigal Son), published in 1636. (Ex. No. 155)

Tempo giusto

So- ha Is- ten há- zá- ra csak ëgy pizt sëm ad- tam.

Ha ja kol- dus tő- lem kért, ha-nyatt ta- szi- tot- tam.

Lan- tost, do- bost, trom- bi- tást mëg- gaz- da- gí- tot- tam,

Ëgy hit- vány, csal- fa csók- ért száz a- ra- nyat ad- tam.

The tune does not exist by itself in the folk-repertory.[122] It is a hitherto unknown contemporary tune of the *Historia* quoted above, as also of the hymn 'Oh, te keresztyén ember' (Oh, thou Christian man), as the textual setting in the first edition would suggest.[123] Can a tune sung at the beginning of the twentieth century be the same as its art-song ancestor of the sixteenth or seventeenth century? The answer could only be given by a contemporary version of the tune, and in most cases this is too much to hope for. But if we consider that people learnt by ear, and that the original unity of words and music strikes deeper and more enduring roots in the memory, we should see nothing strange in the fact that the text has remained linked with the melody for two or three centuries, and that the tune has undergone no essential change.

Here is a seventeenth-century version of a tune from the *Vietorisz MS.* (about 1680) and alongside it two of its variants as they survive today.[124] The text exists in manuscript in several seventeenth-century song-books *(Szencsei MS., Vásárhelyi)*, and also in chapbooks. The Szencsei variant has four lines, the *Vásárhelyi Song-Book* three, while that recorded by Thaly *(Vitézi Énekek*, Vol. II, p. 135) consists of two-line verses with double rhymes. Can all these be fitted to the same tune? The modern folk variant has two lines.

The *Vietorisz MS.* repeats both halves of the tune, and in this way fits the four-line variation. (The *MS.* only gives the opening words of the text.) The three-line variant can be sung to the tune by repeating one half, usually the first. The three forms indicate the widespread popularity of the song, as does its present-day survival.[125]

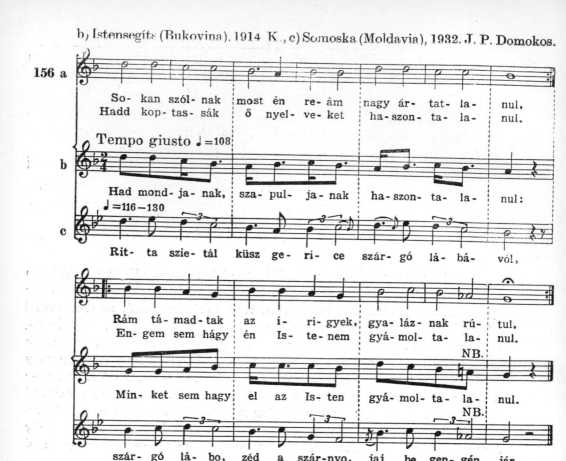

So- kan szól- nak most én re- ám nagy ár- tat- la- nul,
Hadd kop- tas- sák ő nyel- ve- ket ha- szon- ta- la- nul.

Tempo giusto ♩=108

Had mond- ja- nak, sza- pul- ja- nak ha- szon- ta- la- nul:

♩=116—130

Rit- ta szie- tál küsz ge- ri- ce szár- gó lá- bá- vól,

Rám tá- mad- tak az i- ri- gyek, gya- láz- nak rú- tul,
En- gem sem hágy én Is- te- nem gyá- mol- ta- la- nul.

Min- ket sem hagy el az Is- ten gyá- mol- ta- la- nul.

szár- gó lá- bo, zéd a szár- nyo, jaj be gen- gén jár.

'Lupul vajdáné éneke' (Song of the wife of Voivod Lupul), preserved in the *Kájoni MS.* (1634–71)[126] is also recognizable, despite considerable variation, in a folk tune notated

b) Gyergyóalfalu (Csík County), 1911. Antal Molnár

(The text is unknown)

Bú- sulj ró- zsám, mer én sí- rok, Bú- csú- zá- sid rö- vid le- gyen,
Től- led bú- csúz- ni a- ka- rok.

Víg szi- vem- be kárt ne te- gyen, Víg szi-vem-be kárt ne te- gyen.

The melodic curve of the repeated first line is clearly the same, and the unusual five-line song-construction has also been retained. (Repetition of the fourth line has produced the fifth. The original text is unknown.) There is a change in the tune in the third and fourth lines, but the original direction is recognizable at the places marked. The sixth bar is probably a mistake; the upward leap to the seventh may be accounted for by the usual octave change (see p. 68). If lower *f* is read for upper *f*, the folk variant is brought closer to the original tune.

Who knows how many Hungarian tunes may not be settings of old Hungarian lyrics? Or how many unidentified tunes may not conceal 'historical songs,' rhyming chronicles and versified short stories, more particularly in dodecasyllabic verse recitative? (See Exs. Nos. 63 and 69, and the following tunes Nos. 158 and 159.)

Lédec (Bars County), 1907. K.

158

Parlando ♩=100

Jaj, de szë- rën- csét- len i- dő- re ju- tot- tam!

Ez csa- lárd vi- lág- ba mind- ad- dig jád- szot- tam,

Ez csa- lárd vi- lág- ba mind- ad- dig jád- szot- tam,

I- ri- gyek nyel- vé- re jaj, de rá- ju- tot- tam.

Szárhegy (Csík County), 1910. K.

159

Rubato ♩= cca 76−80

Ma- gas Dé- va vá- rát é- pi- te- ni kezd- ték,

An- nak é- lit- ü- gyét sem- mi- be se lel- ték.

A- kit rëg- gel rak- tak, a' dél- be el- om- lott,

115

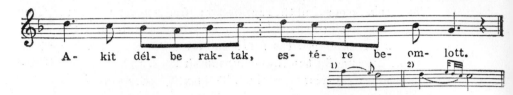

A- kit dél- be rak- tak, es- té- re be- om- lott.

Some of these are stylistically related to analogous examples of old Hungarian art-music:[127] the tunes of the so-called 'beggars' songs,' for instance, are often reminiscent.[128]

Andrásfalva (Bukovina), 1914. K.

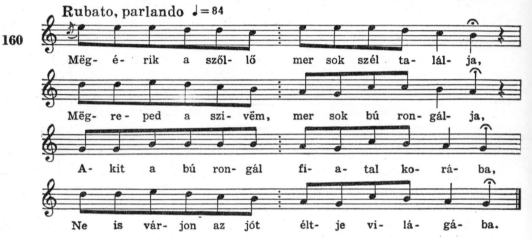

Rubato, parlando ♩=84

160

Mëg- é- rik a sző̈l- lő mer sok szél ta- lál- ja,

Mëg- re- ped a szi- vëm, mer sok bú ron- gál- ja,

A- kit a bú ron- gál fi- a- tal ko- rá- ba,

Ne is vár- jon az jót élt- je vi- lá- gá- ba.

Even their texts seem to be effete descendants of the 'historical songs.'[129]

Ecseg (Nógrád County), 1922. K.

Parlando ♩=92

161

Si- ral- mas ez vi- lág ne- künk bű- nö- sök- nek,

Ha jól mëg- gon- dol- juk nap- ját é- le- tünk- nek.

Mert már el- me- rül- tünk a nagy ke- vil- síg- be,

Jaj lëssz az é- le- tünk si- ra- lom völ- gyé- be.

The eight verses of this song contain moralizing reflections on the famine of 1866 and end with a prayer. The tune is related to that of the *Prodigal Son* previously quoted (No. 155) (lines 3 and 4).

From the beginning, interdependence of text and tune in epic songs was less marked; even in the first editions textual alternatives are given and in later editions, entirely different versions. Yet in editions of the verse stories of *Argirus,* the original text is faithfully retained; even the last one gives the original *ad notam* 'Oly búval bánattal az Aeneas király' (With such sorrow did King Aeneas...)—the first line of a Hungarian version of the *Aeneid,* dating from 1582.

Sometimes the tune of the lyric was changed, too, particularly if people had the text in printed form. Those who had never heard the poem sung then tried to set it to any tune.

Thus it is that András Janóczi's 'Ideje bujdosásimnak'[130] (The time has come for me to flee) and 'Ifjúság mint sólyom madár'[131] (Youth, like a falcon) have been found with many different tunes. Both occur several times in eighteen-century chapbooks.

Gyergyóújfalu (Csík County), 1907. B.

162

Lédec (Bars County), 1907. K.

163

Although István Dobai's song (see No. 152) is also found in chapbooks, it has come down to us with only one tune. Its more unusual verse form (6, 6, 8, 8) may have made a change of tune more difficult. It is likely that it is the original tune that has been preserved, both by the peasantry and in Ádám Pálóczi-Horváth's manuscript.

These observations set in relief a particularly important feature of Hungarian folk-tradition. It has preserved a few remnants of musical settings of sixteenth and seventeenth-century Hungarian lyrics—some of the loveliest poetry that Hungary possesses. In the absence of contemporary musical records, scarcely anything would otherwise be known of such songs. Folk-tradition shows how these must have sounded in living performance, of which only an incomplete idea can be formed from the imperfect notations of a few tunes.[132]

Further research will make clear whether these folk remains relate to Hungarian or to foreign art-music. International dances of the day were also taken over (there are traces of them in all Hungarian manuscripts), and when more is known of them, their traces will also be found in Hungarian folk-tradition. As for the tune of the 'Volta,'[133] a dance that spread like an epidemic in the sixteenth century, it seems likely that traces of it appear in the following folk tune:

Berencs (Nyitra County), 1909. K.

164

A-rany, e- züst-ért, cif- ra ru- há-ért, Le-ányt el ne végy ko-szo- rú- já-ért.

In-kább sze- res-sed jám-bor-sá-gá-ért, E- lőt-ted va-ló szép já- rá- sá-ért.

This tune is still to be found in many parts of Hungary, especially in its half-size, eight-bar variants, which correspond to the 'Volta' in range as well. One of them is the well-known song for children's singing games 'Kis kacsa fürdik' (A little duck is swimming).[134]

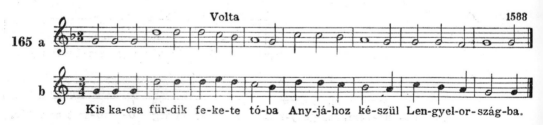

Volta   1588

165 a

b

Kis ka-csa für-dik fe-ke-te tó-ba Any-já-hoz ké-szül Len-gyel-or-szág-ba.

There is much scope for research into these migrant motifs from earlier periods; but in the meantime there is also much to discover about the origin of more recent tunes. For example: the tune of 'Én vagyok a petri gulyás' (I am the herdsman from Petri) occurs, as early as 1765, in a mythological play of the Order of St. Paul in Újhely.[135]

118

The following tune is found in István Gáti's *Piano Tutor* (1802) with the title 'Magyar Aria a *Quodlibet* operából, Kótsi Úrtól'[136] (Hungarian Air from the opera *Quodlibet*, by Mr. Kótsi). The folk variant is from Füzesgyarmat (Hont County), 1912, Z. Kodály. It is noticeable that the tune of the second verse differs from that of the first. Folk singers have even managed to retain such complicated constructions as this:

There is a curious tune, quoted by Bartók (No. 270), which differs from the main type of folksong both in construction and melodic line:

Magyargyerőmonostor (Kolozs County), 1910. B.

Ö- kör- sze- kér a ka- pu- ba, a vő- le- gény az aj- tó- ba,

A meny- asz- szony az ab- lak- ba.

It has five lines; its use of intervals resembles late eighteenth-century art-songs; the principal caesura on the major third points to a foreign origin. In Transylvania, it plays a part in marriage festivities, and is sung when the bride is fetched. *Ethnographia* (1915, p. 141) gives it as 'an old Székely bridal song' from Udvarhely County. Apart from this, it is known only in Gömör County, as a drinking song. The words of the Gömör text can be recognized in the two lines noted by István Tóth in his manuscript collection (1832–43). Here, too, the original was a drinking song, though not a word of the text was retained by peasant singers (text by Endre Horváth, set to music by József Silberknoll, published as an appendix in the journal *Tudományos Gyűjtemény*, 1824, No. 3). Here are the three tunes one below the other; the original at the top (Ex. No. 168a), below it István Tóth's variant (b), and at the bottom the folksong (c) (Gömör County, 1912, Z. Kodály; cf. Bartalus, Vol. IV, No. 11).

c) Perjése (Gömör County), 1912. K.

Original final **Sotto voce**

168 a

Nem kell né-kem sem Czipru-si, sem a vö-rös Bur- gun-di, Sem raj-na- i,

b

I-gyál ſzép ſzó, fi-zess nem jó, Ez az i- ga- zi Magyar szó *(there is no further text)*

c

I-gyál Pét-ro fizess: něm jó, Ez az i- ga- zi ma-gyar szó! Ha nincs bankó,

Ma- la- ga- i, Hi-szem Is- te- ne-met, Nem he- vít en- ge-met.

van ə réz-kongó, Itt ma-radt a kan-kó De ȷaz něm i-gěn jó.

120

The influence of art-music has been a continuous process, and each age has added a fresh stratum. Sometimes this cannot be clearly seen today, owing to the lack of written records. The last stage in this process was that in which nineteenth-century popular art-song merged with the folk-tradition. We saw it happen with our own eyes, and the detailed observation that was then possible promises well for study of the more distant past. Such systematic research can only be undertaken through the great tune-collection of the Hungarian Academy, the *Corpus Musicae Popularis Hungaricae*, now in course of publication.

'FLOWER SONGS'*

The term *virágének* (flower song) is unknown to the folk vocabulary, but this type of song has certainly not died out, save in name. Where is it to be found today?

For centuries, priests of every confession are known to have attacked the flower songs (or secular love songs) and tried to eradicate them. What did they find so objectionable? As cultivated men of letters, were they as insensitive to poetry when led by Péter Pázmány, the great leader of the Counter-Reformation? The Humanist preacher, János Erdősi Sylvester, suggests the very opposite. His words (1541) are often quoted in part, but deserve to be given in full. He apologizes for comparing this 'Hungarian poetry,' the flower songs, with the language of the Bible, and goes on: 'When I make use of such a humble example in such exalted matters, I am seeking gold in the dung; it is not that I approve such vanities. I do not praise the content of these songs: I praise the noble art of their expression.'[137] He was praising the style, not the subject. The 'dung' can only be taken to mean the open praise of physical love. This was the object of his attack, not language akin to that of the Bible.

In our own day there are many folksongs that deal with erotic aspects of life in a completely uninhibited way.[138] They are common to every people, and form one of the flourishing branches of 'primitive poetry.' Scientific research classifies them apart as *cryptadia*. The modern concept of morality and social decency has followed the view of the Churches and opposed them. But in the sixteenth century they did not rouse great moral indignation. A glance at a contemporary French or German song-collection suffices to prove this. The songs were current among the humbler classes as well as at royal courts: the greatest composers (for example, Orlando di Lasso) set them to music, in more refined form perhaps, but handling their subject with even more sophisticated candour.

* XVIth—XVIIth-century lyric songs with floral symbolism.

Some Hungarian peasants still retain this older concept of decency and are not to be censured for it. It goes with a simpler emotional life, more direct and natural. In most districts, however, a majority of the peasants consider such songs indecent and do not easily disclose them.

But the *virágének* cannot have been pure *cryptadia*. The name came from songs that repeatedly mention flowers and refer to lovers by the names of flowers. Peasants know many such songs, the descendants of the original flower songs. The richness of the song-type is revealed in an unbroken line from the time of the citation of Péter Melius Juhász's three flower songs (1561),[139] of the Sopron fragment (pre-1495) and even earlier, up to the present.

The type with refrain deserves special notice. The Sopron fragment[140] too, may be a refrain:

> Virág, tudjad, tűled el kell mennem
> És te íretted kell gyászba öltöznem.

> (Flower, thou know'st I must leave thee,
> And for thy sake put on mourning.)

—like its modern counterpart:

> Virágom, véled elmegyek,
> Virágom, tőled el sem maradok.

> (My flower, I'll go with you,
> My flower, I'll never leave you.)

Ghymes (Nyitra County), 1906. K.[141]

169

Ve- te- kë- gyik vé- lem hã- rom- fé- le vi- rág,

Vi- rá- gom, vé- led e- lə-më- gyëk

vi- rá- gom, tő- led e- lə sëm mã.- rà- dok.

It is possible to make a lovely garland of flower refrains. Here are a few examples:

Nagypeszek (Hont County), 1912. K.

Tempo giusto

170

Te-li ker-tem zsá-lyá-val szép a legény párjával Gyöngyöm vi-olám a-ra-nyos almám

Mohi (Bars County), 1912. K.

171

Te-li ker-tëm zsá-lyá-val Szíp a legény párjával. *R:* Gyën-ge vi-olám Szíp arany almám

Karád (Somogy County), 1934. Gy. Dávid.

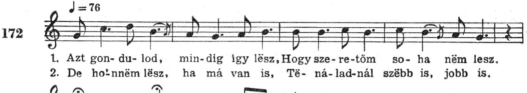

172

1. Azt gon- du- lod,   min-dig igy lësz, Hogy sze-re-tőm so- ha nëm lesz.
2. De ho-nnëm lësz, ha má van is, Të- ná-lad-nál szëbb is, jobb is.

R: Haj, rú- zsa, haj, he- je, hu- ja, haj.

Zsére (Nyitra County), 1906. K.

173

Ci- pël- lő szá- jó ke-víl më-nyasz-szony! Szíp bacskor szájú ke-víl vő- le- gíny!

R: Rú-zsa szi-vem, rú- zsa lel- këm   haj, vi- rá- gom,   haj!

The next example is used in the Zobor region of Nyitra to waken the newly-married couple the day after the wedding. It also occurs as a variant in the collection of Gábor Mátray (1852–54), No. 71:

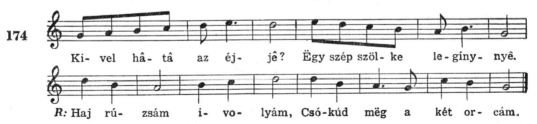

174

Ki- vel hâ- tâ az éj- jê? Ëgy szép szöl- ke   le- gíny- nyê.

R: Haj rú- zsám   i- vo- lyám, Csó-kúd mëg a két or- cám.

An example of a longer refrain occurs in Kriza's collection:

Szerelmes virág, szerelmes virág,
Nincsen annál szebb kincs,
Kinek szíve bánatban nincsen, nincsen, nincs.[142]

(Lovelorn flowers, lovelorn flowers,
There's no more precious treasure
Than a heart that's never, never, never filled with sorrow.)

Later it was also discovered with a melody:

CMPH IV, No. 605. Lengyelfalva (Udvarhely County), 1903. V.

175

Ëggy asz-szony-na-kə va- la há-rom lë- á- nya:

Sze- rel- me- şə vi- rág, sze- rel- me- şə vi- rág.

Nin- csen an-nál szëbb kincs, ki-nek szí-ve bá-nat-ba Nin-csen, nin-csen, nincs.

The refrain is not at all frequent in Hungarian folksong. It seems possible that it came via the Middle Ages of Western Europe, from the rich tradition of refrain poetry which flourished so remarkably in France. It is certain that occasional foreign influences had already begun to penetrate folk-tradition by Sylvester's time (sixteenth century). The learned preacher discusses the metaphorical phrases used by the peasants in their speech, and admires the 'inventive wit of the Hungarian populace,' that is, not that of the nobility or of the poets. He would certainly have made it clear had he meant verses of literary origin.[143] It is obvious that he had also heard other types of song from peasant singers, since he gives pride of place to the *virágének* as a poetic form—'especially in the "virágének," ' he writes.

Let us join him in admiring the 'gold' that he saw in the 'dung,' and the peasants who have preserved it for the delight of us all.

VIII INSTRUMENTAL MUSIC

For a long time it seemed that the Hungarian people had no particular affection for instrumental music—a belief encouraged by the small number of 'classical' folk instruments—zither, bagpipe, short and long shepherd's pipes, swineherd's horn and hurdy-gurdy—and by the fact that even these had appeared to be on the way to extinction from the time when the collection of folksong began. Only the notable spread of the zither throughout the country, and its evident popularity, might have given cause for re-consideration of this belief.

As the result of the investigations of Bálint Sárosi, an entirely new picture has emerged.[144] On the basis of his own collections, and through the assessment of data stemming from earlier, scattered sources (chiefly from ethnographers), he has been able to demonstrate the existence of an exceptionally rich stock of instruments. A large number of primitive sound-producing implements for special occasions has been brought to light, together with variants of the classical instruments made from uncommon materials (sunflower stalks, gourds, and gourd stems), and various 'modern' innovations. This abundance, recorded throughout the country, and the observed demand for factory-made instruments and for opportunities for instrumental study, together indicate that the Hungarian people are by no means indifferent to instrumental music. In many regions, peasant bands have recently come into existence, sometimes consisting of wind instruments only, but mostly using the mixture of instruments common to gipsy bands. Pleasure in musical sounds produced by different instruments has followed the Hungarians throughout their history from the traditional forms of a subsistence economy, to the newer possibilities offered by the development of urban civilization. One of the most interesting manifestations of this kind is to be observed among the herdsmen, who represent the most archaic heritage; most herdsmen select the large and small bells for their herds in such a way that their sounds are in harmony together. They spare neither effort nor material sacrifice in order to obtain a needed and appropriate bell. In 1963, an old herdsman boasted that '... when in the dewy morning he drove his cows (wearing tinkling bells) well tuned, it sounded like divine service. Even the Holy Mass didn't come up to it.' (Sárosi, p. 20.)

Since these recent findings are available to Western readers in German, we shall not attempt to deal here with the complete Hungarian instrumentarium. Nor shall we deal with the traditional dance-music practice of Transylvanian gipsy bands, now beginning to become familiar from recent recordings, as yet incompletely studied. It will suffice to mention the commonest instruments and the music played on them.

FOLK INSTRUMENTS

There are home-made instruments such as the Jew's harp *(doromb)*, swineherd's horn *(kanásztülök)*, herdsman's horn *(pásztorkürt)*, short and long shepherd's pipe *(furulya)*, bagpipe *(duda)*, zither *(citera)* or cittern *(tambura)*; less common instruments are the dulcimer or cymbalum *(cimbalom)*, hurdy-gurdy *(tekerő* or *nyenyere)*, that is the French *vielle* (see Plate facing p. 81); and there are manufactured instruments such as violin, clarinet, cymbalum, bugle, accordion and mouth-organ.

It is for the student of musical folklore to discover what peasants play. Art-music can be played on home-made instruments, just as folk music can be played on manufactured instruments. Ethnography deals with the description of the instruments and their construction.[145] Folk-music research examines their technique and range, insofar as this is necessary to understand the music performed on them.

Gipsies. It is a much debated question whether gipsy music-making should rank as folk music. The ethnographical importance of the gipsy musician lies in what he knows over and above the song and dance music of the towns. When he plays folk music, he is relevant to the subject. A considerable quantity of dance music, the origin of which is at present unknown, is to be heard from gipsies in Transylvania. Peasants use it for dancing, but never sing or play it themselves. The gipsy is thus the sole source.

There is a difference in the way peasants feel about songs and instrumental music. Even in the song-tradition, all do not have equal shares. There is a sharp distinction between active and passive types. There are independent, leading singers who know much and know it well; there are others who will join in if someone starts, but are uncertain by themselves; there are 'one-song' people. There is the passive type who does not sing but only listens; he knows the songs, and knows them so well that he will notice mistakes, but he never utters a note (except perhaps when drunk).

Where instrumental music is concerned, however, everyone is a listener; performance is the task of a few. Whether the musician is a gipsy or a peasant, he stands alone, or with a few companions, face to face with the listening masses. These are not entirely passive: they dance to the music and are quick to feel if it is not played to their liking. They are critical and discriminating and can distinguish what is good. In 1910, a young village gipsy in Transylvania said it was hardest of all to play to the old Székely—a young gipsy could never really do it as they wanted.

Hence, in instrumental folk music, peasants have long since strayed away from the original lines of folk-culture—a state of musical self-sufficiency. At a pinch, young people will dance to a sung accompaniment, but dancing cannot take place at a village gathering, however humble, without instruments and invited musicians. Peasants never pay for what they themselves produce (for them 'bought bread' or 'bought linen' are unthinkable). It is, however, an old and deeply-rooted custom to recompense the musical contribution to dance and wedding celebrations. Here the paid specialist is already in existence: the professional expert has been substituted for 'home industry.'

Whether the musician is able to live off this payment is another question. Under more primitive conditions it seems to have been impossible. In 1912, I was present when a well-to-do Székely farmer engaged a gipsy to play at his son's wedding; he was the only musician in Kászonfeltíz, a place of some 10,000 inhabitants. This single fiddler had to play for twenty-four hours in return for food and drink, some kerchiefs and five forints (then about 10 shillings). Naturally, he could not live on this. His main occupation was that of a smith, so he was called away from his anvil into the bargain.[146] Such unpretentiousness—on both sides—is perhaps surprising; popular fancy imagines sizable bands of gipsies in even the smallest village. It should be realized, however, that as long ago as the 1880s, they 'made do' in quite a number of places (Garam Valley, Félegyháza) with a single bagpiper even for a well-to-do wedding. Gipsy musicians at that time preferred to confine themselves to the outskirts of provincial towns. Just as the country people increasingly tended to ape 'genteel' ways, so the gipsies gradually spread to small villages where they had never been seen before. This radiation of gipsy skill must have tended to reduce still further the peasants' taste for music-making. In more ambitious areas, the solitary fiddler was joined by one, or more rarely two, second fiddlers.[147]

Later on, even in small villages, the cymbalum, clarinet, cello and double-bass were regarded as indispensable. In the 1830s even a Transylvanian magnate like Miklós Wesselényi was content with four gipsies.[148] The same instruments were used when folk orchestras ('Magyar bands') were formed after the model of gipsy bands. Normally, however, folk instrumental music differs sharply from the gipsy variety in style as in choice of instruments. The gipsy never uses the zither, shepherd's pipe, bagpipe, accordion, Jew's harp or hurdy-gurdy. The herdsman's horn (made of bark) and swineherd's horn are tools of trades rather than musical instruments, though some players manage to give them musical interest; see for instance Exs. Nos. 176 and 177.[149]

Environment of Ipolyság (Hont County), 1911. B.

Violin, cymbalum and clarinet are commonly used both by gipsy and peasant musicians. Cornet and clarinet were introduced to peasant communities by the brass bands that have recently begun to spread in Hungarian villages. The clarinet is sometimes used as a solo instrument away from the orchestra.

Zither (citera). The most widespread folk-instrument is the home-made zither. There are two types, the diatonic and the chromatic, to be distinguished at a glance. On the finger board *(kótafa)* of the diatonic zither there are frets *(kóta)* under the strings *(kótahúr)* (two sets of two, or two sets of three) on which the tune is played; these are stretched over the slightly raised bottom edge of the finger board. Thus all four (or 6–7) melody strings produce the same scale (usually d_1-b_2, and on larger instruments an even higher pitched Mixolydian scale).* The scale can be read from the illustration (Plate facing p. 17), as the distance between the frets indicates the position of the whole notes and semitones.

The two pairs of melody strings of the chromatic zither have different frets. The fret under the outer pair of strings produces the Mixolydian scale (usually d_1-g_3, or, less frequently, three complete octaves to d_4). The inner pair provides the missing chromatic notes: $d_1\sharp$ (sometimes missing, see Plate facing p. 17), f_1-$g_1\sharp$-$b_1\flat$-$c_2\sharp$, etc.

A skilled chromatic-zither player can perform songs and any other kind of music *(csárdás*, dances, Rákóczi march) permitted by the technique of the instruments. Large jumps in quick tempi are difficult. The tuning of the accompanying sympathetic or 'guest' strings *(vendéghúrok)* is interesting. On a diatonic zither, all accompaniment strings are usually tuned d_1, and a thicker one to d. On a chromatic zither the tunings are variable and more complicated, being connected with the shape of the instrument. Apart from the rectangular or curved-sided instrument, the 'puppy-headed' *(kölyökfejes)* or 'small-headed' instrument is often found on the Alföld (Hungarian Plain). The 'large head' *(nagyfej)* is in the centre, ending in a snail or a horse's head. On the right side are fixed one to three small heads decreasing in size, carved in the same way as the large head. These small heads each carry one, two, or three strings, each of which is tuned higher than the preceding one. An instrument from Túrkeve, with three small heads, is tuned as follows: the first string of the large head is g, and is called *kisbőgő* (little *contrebasse)*, the others being d and D (thicker, overwound string): this latter is the *nagybőgő* (big *contrebasse)*. The small heads are tuned: 1 g_1, 2 d_2, 3 g_2. The use of the small heads is unknown; it seems that a good player touches them now and again when they fit into the harmony, but a poorer exponent does not use them at all. The music of a good zither player will fill a room, and zithers are sometimes used to accompany dances.

---

* In diatonic notation this is a major scale with a flattened seventh. (Translator's note.)

The basic Mixolydian scale of zithers and shepherds' pipes is definitely related to the importance of the scale in new-style Hungarian folksongs. Songs in other scales are transposed to different degrees of this scale. This procedure throws an interesting light on the nascent sense of harmony. Ex. No. 178a, b, represents a tune as sung and as performed on the zither in the same village.[150]

Zabar (Gömör County), 1907. K.

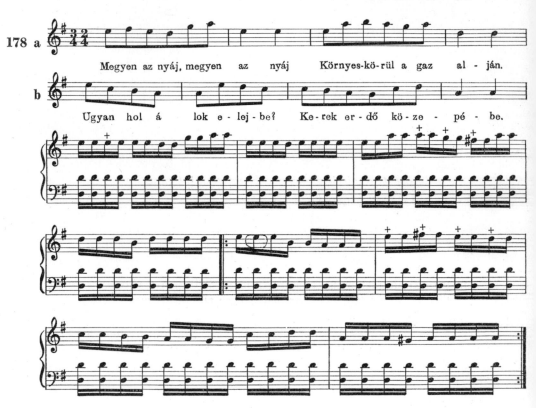

It is striking that even after several singings and playings *precisely the deviation marked with + remained*, whereas at Zabar I did not hear this form of the song *sung*. It is unfortunate that so little is known about this. Generally speaking, folk skill and folk customs in instrumental playing have so far received scant attention. No comparison has yet been made between the construction and tuning of the home-made peasant zither and the industrial zither so popular in Austria.

Shepherd's pipe (furulya). Peasants have two types of shepherd's pipe. On the *long type* (about 93 cm. or 3 ft.) there are five holes near the bottom, so that it can only be played with the head held very high. (Plates facing pp. 49 and 64). The keynote is *f* or *e*. The scale is:[151]

130

179

The third note is sometimes too low, only a minor third from the fundamental. The fundamental series is not used, probably because of the gap between *c* and *f*. The bracketed notes can be blown, but we have never heard them used. The instrument is becoming rarer and is now only to be found in Southern Transdanubia. Several very fine ornamented examples are to be seen in the Budapest Ethnographical Museum. (See Plates facing pp. 17 and 33.)

The common six-holed pipe exists in many sizes. The length varies between 30 cm. and 60 cm. (1 to 2 ft.) and the keynote between c_1 and d_2. In some places, the smaller ones are called *pikula* (piccolo). In addition to the normal type, made of maple or elder, there are smaller ones made from copper tubing or even from the stem of hemlock. Here again the fundamental series is not normally used, so that in practice the range is of one or one-and-a-half octaves. In rare cases, it is shaped like a flute, the upper end closed, and blown through a hole in the side.

Fundamental Series   *Overtones 1*   *Overtones 2*   *Overtones 3*

180

The scale approximates to the major or Mixolydian, but by half-covering some holes, it is possible to play minor tunes.

The following example (No. 181) shows the practice-runs of a pipe player in Hont County. The keynote is g_1, and he uses the Mixolydian scale through two octaves. Then he plays a tune (given with words on p. 24, Ex. No. 1) in which $b\flat$ and $e\flat$ also occur. (For the same tune performed on the bagpipe, see p. 136, Ex. No. 186; on the violin, p. 137, Ex. No. 188):

181

Tunes with an octave range do not usually begin on the keynote of the instrument, but on the fourth, as in Ex. No. 180 above. Transylvanian pipe players frequently begin minor tunes on the second degree because in pentatonic tunes they need no notes below the lower second. For the rest, the breaking of the melodic line by transposition at an octave, usual in singing (see p. 68), is normal for the pipe as well, even though rarer.

It is a curious custom of pipe players (especially in Transylvania) to hum or growl some deep note into the pipe while playing. As this spoils the clarity of the higher notes, we attempted to stop them from doing this in recordings. They were so used to it, that to stop them was difficult if not impossible. The humming accompaniment is meant to imitate the bagpipe's drone, and forms harmonic effects with the notes of the pipe, so that a third part can often be heard. In Pátria record No. 59A, the melody is played on a long pipe. The notation (Ex. No. 182) is by Bartók, see *Magyar Népzenei Gramofonfelvételek. Az Országos Történeti Museum Néprajzi Osztályának felvételei (Gramophone Recordings of Hungarian Folk Music.* Recordings of the Ethnographic Department of the National Historical Museum. Series 1. 1937.) The growling is to be heard throughout the performance, but the notation shows only notes of definite pitch:

Berzence (Somogy County).

Clever players are no rarity even today, but they do not achieve the decorative artistry or the repertory of the old performers.

Bagpipe (duda). In common with other instrumentalists, the bagpiper has never made a living from his instrument. Players were generally shepherds, to be found for the most part in Transdanubia, Northern Hungary and Csallóköz. At a horn and bagpipe concert in Ipolyság in 1911 (Plate facing p. 16), the district was still able to provide bagpipers. In other areas, even when old bagpipers were still alive, their instruments lay idle and desiccated. At most they played for children's dances, if such existed, but adults looked down on them, and would have been ashamed to dance to the instrument. Since the First World War, however, more and more has been heard of the revival of bagpipe playing. In 1934, at a meeting of the Budapest Ethnographical Society, a bagpiper from Northern Hungary played his instrument to illustrate a lecture by L. Madarassy.[152] When folk music began to be recorded in 1938, active bagpipers could still be found in Hungary. According to Madarassy, it was post-war poverty in the Palóc district which brought the instrument back into fashion.

Described by a seventeenth-century preacher as 'the foremost musical instrument of the Magyars,'[153] it was inherited by Rumanians in Transylvania as part of the shepherd tradition. In the seventeenth century it was a favourite instrument of the Transylvanian Prince Apafi, but has since gone out of fashion to such an extent that from about 1900 onwards Hungarian bagpipers have been almost unheard of in that area. (See, however, above for the revival of the bagpipe in Hungary.)

The bagpiper always plays by himself; as the proverb has it: 'Two bagpipers in the same inn don't mix.' Sometimes the tune is played on a shepherd's pipe also, together with the bagpipe, but two bagpipes cannot be tuned together: each has a different pitch.

The shape of the bagpipe is not different now from that in a drawing of 1816 (Plate facing p. 80). This drawing makes it clear that recruiting drives *(verbunkos)* had no need of gipsies because of the popularity of the bagpipe amongst the peasants; this is substantiated by many documents and by a quantity of bagpipe tunes. In the illustration, a devil is carved on the end of the drone pipe. Such instruments are no longer to be seen, but János Arany's ballad 'Ünneprontók' (Sabbath-breakers) is based on a folk legend about a demon bagpiper.

In addition to goat or ram-headed bagpipes, some museums on the Alföld (Szentes, Szeged) have bagpipes with heads of young girls or men. Nothing is known of their origin, and they have never been seen in the hands of Hungarian, Slovak or Rumanian pipers (with the exception of that from Kiskunhalas seen by Vargyas, mentioned in Note No. 152). It is still debatable whether they are of Hungarian or other origin (Plate facing p. 81).

No historical data on pitch or scale are available. Their tuning varies. The fundamental series is between f and $b\flat$. We have also heard Serbian bagpipes in d. The considerable amount of wind necessary for the lower notes may explain why Serbian pipers—like Italians and Scotsmen—tend to use bellows. The Hungarian bagpiper always blows up his bag with his mouth, without using a bellows (save the Kiskunhalas piper, Note No. 152).

The *sípszár* (pipe-holder) comprises two high pipes, usually carved out of one piece of plum-wood. The chanter has seven holes, the accompaniment-pipe one. The goat's head covers the simple clarinet-like single-beating reed of both, cut from a reed. The arrangement of the pipes varies. Generally (and always in Upper Hungary and Slovakia) the seven-hole tube is on the left of the piper. Very rarely (as in the bagpipe on the Plate facing p. 32, from Somogy County or Croatia) the single-hole tube is in this position. From this it may be inferred that the Plate facing p. 65 shows a Hungarian bagpiper.

The rear hole next to the bagpiper's thumb is called the 'first.' The opposite hole is called the 'changer' *(váltó);* it is bored in a slightly raised part of the pipe and is a good deal narrower than the others. The 'second' hole is covered by the middle finger and the 'third' by the fourth finger. The next hole is the 'contra' for which the second hand is used. The 'changer' is operated by the little finger and is the only sound-producing aperture of the accompaniment tube.

This description of the bagpipe's mechanism was given to me in 1922 by Péter Szabó, a seventy-year-old herdsman from Szuha (Karancsság). According to László Madarassy's more recent researches, the little hole at the top of the 'prime-tube' *(prímcső)* is called 'flea-hole' *(bolhaluk)*—'it produces a flattened sound when closed'—and is used for ornamentation; the 'shouting-hole' *(fölkiáltóluk)* 'produces a high note'; then comes the 'second-hole' *(másodikluk)* which 'produces a high note,' the 'change-hole' *(váltóluk)*, the 'counter-balancer' *(kontraegyenlítő)* and the 'note-player' *(hangjátszó)*. The inner hole is called 'screamer-hole' *(sikajtóluk)* and produces a screaming note. The contra-tube hole *(kontracső)* is the 'contra-hole' *(kontraluk)*. The names are significant: the 'screamer' has the highest note at the octave. The 'middle-note' is the fifth, that is, the octave of the keynote of the 'contra-tube.' Such names throw light on the way in which peasants formulate their musical ideas, about which very little is known. The drone-pipe is usually composed of four parts and produces a single note; it is the 'drone' *(bordó* or *gordó)*.

The scale of the tune-pipe is usually Mixolydian. By opening the 'flea-hole' it is possible to raise the lower notes by a semitone. It is seldom used, generally only for the minor third and for a few short trills. Less experienced players keep it permanently blocked with wax, in which case the scale is incomplete: g, a_1, b_1, c_2, d_2, e_2, g_2. Occasionally a faultily bored pipe gives the major seventh instead of the octave, and sometimes the sixth is missing: g_1, a_1, b_1, c_2, d_2, f_2, $(f\sharp)$, g_2.

Following Madarassy's exhaustive, detailed description of the Palóc bagpipes, detailed work on the bagpipe and other folk-instruments is clearly needed both from the point of view of acoustics and of the history of the instrument, and from that of comparative study of folk-instruments of neighbouring peoples.[154]

Hurdy-gurdy (nyenyere or *tekerő)*. Like the bagpipe, the hurdy-gurdy (see Plates facing pp. 81 and 96) used to be an international instrument.[155] In Hungary there are traces of it at Szentes. One of the last specimens was made about 1907 by J. Szerényi, who has since died. (Information kindly supplied by Gábor Csallány, then Curator of Szentes District Museum.) His son, however, is still alive and plays his own hand-made instrument. This was described by Béla Bartók, who also published the tunes played on it.[156] Even as late as 1939 it was possible to find a hurdy-gurdy player for the Pátria gramophone recordings (Nos. 52–56). Its heritage survived, however, and the instrument has recently been revived. In 1960 a man living in the neighbourhood of Szentes made a hurdy-gurdy for the Budapest Ethnographical Museum, and it has recently come into use again in folk ensembles. (Bagpipe recordings are to be found on Pátria records 5 and 7–9, and shepherd's pipe recordings on records 12, 13, 26, 51 and 59.)

WHAT PEASANTS PLAY ON THEIR INSTRUMENTS

For the most part, songs are dressed up in instrumental guise. The repertory includes pieces performed without text, but with a construction and style most likely to have originated from songs. Only one has been discovered in which the shepherd's pipe plays an essential part. It can also be sung without the pipe, but this is incorrect.

At dead of night, three ruffians break into a miller's house and say 'Miller, where's your money?' 'My money's in the drawer, only spare my life.':

183

Mó-nár, hun a pén-zëd? zëd? „Subla-tom-ba van a pénzëm,Csak az é-le-tëmet féltëm.

Then he asks them to let him play a tune on his pipe for the last time. When they give him permission, he calls his dogs as follows (the part in brackets is sung only when there is no pipe, hence without ornamentation):

184

Jam-bor⟩[gyere ha- za!]　Héjsze[bum,bum,gyere haza!Héjsze bum,bum,gyere ha-za]
Fok-tor⟨

The dogs hear it and run home. When they reach the courtyard, the miller plays:

185

So the dogs run in and tear the three ruffians to bits.

Up to now, this has only been known from several Transdanubian variants. Two variants occur in the new series of ethnological recordings (Pátria records 24 and 29). The French and Bulgarian variants of the story are sung throughout to a melody.[157] In the Bulgarian song, the herdsman summons his dogs for help with his pipe in the same way as our miller. The melodic 'insert' seems to be the last vestige of a melody of long ago current among the Hungarians. In type it recalls the 'goat-song' of Rumanian pipe players and fiddlers, known in countless variants and even mentioned in the sixteenth century by Bálint Balassa: the goatherd mourns the loss of his goats, then exults as he thinks he sees them, but the objects seen are only rocks; he relapses into sadness, but at last finds them, expressing his joy in a gay dance tune.

It is very interesting to compare the second half of the tune in its sung and instrumental form. The tune is modified because the pipe has no seventh. In its place the first, and sometimes the fourth, is used. This is a typical folk-music procedure, if the tune goes beyond the range of the instrument. For the most part, essentials are cleverly preserved.

The following example is the same as the song given on p. 24, Ex. No. 1 as performed by a bagpiper. The a_2 of the tune has been lost, because the bagpipe only has an octave range.

Hont County, 1911. B.

186

Since folk-instruments are primarily used for dances, the tunes played on them are generally suitable for dancing; but slow, sad tunes are also played, particularly on the shepherd's pipe. The tune given with text on p. 56, Ex. No. 69 is played here on the pipe:

Nyárád-Köszvényes
(Maros-Torda County), Transylvania, 1914. B.

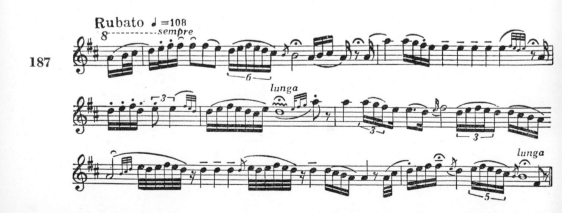

187

It is not easy to distinguish the simple sung tune from the runs of the *furulya*. But such comparisons help to explain the instrumental style of folk music. Even dance tunes are sometimes concealed in instrumental figures, though not to the same extent as are the slow 'lamenting songs.'

Some Rumanian authorities hold that the themes in my *Marosszék Dances*, based on Transylvanian dance tunes, are in fact Rumanian dances. The only evidence brought forward is half a tune in Kálmán Chován's *Rumanian Dances*. The title is not always decisive; gipsies are responsible for much confusion. In some places, Bukovina for instance, they play to four or five nationalities. The following violin piece (a variant of the well-known Hungarian song given on p. 24, Ex. No. 1) was called 'Ardeleana' (that is, Transylvanian) by its performer, a Hungarian peasant from Bukovina. But there are numerous well-known Rumanian dance pieces with the same name but quite differently constructed. Dance tunes with similar rhythms are easily exchanged between peoples: Hungarians will dance Hungarian dances, and Rumanians Rumanian dances to the same pieces of music.[158]

188

Of greater importance is the language of the text. In another study I have compared[159] the tune in question (the principal theme of my *Marosszék Dances*) with a Hungarian song never sung by Rumanians, though traces of it can be followed up. Carefully examined, the tune is a modern variant of a 'flower song,' preserved in manuscript form in the *Vietorisz Virginal Book* (c. 1680).[160] Its text occurs in seventeenth-century manuscripts (*Vásárhelyi Song-Book*, *Mátray MS.* and *Komárom Song-Book*).[161] The mistakes in rhythm made by the amateur scribe as he noted it down are not surprising.

In parallel with this old form (Ex. No. 189a) and the new instrumental version (No. 189b), I quoted a modern variant with text from Csíksomlyó (Coll. P. Domokos, No. 189c). When modern variants are formed, it is not unusual for the second half of the tune to be a note, and later a fifth, lower. The original ABBA form of the tune (obviously a composed variant) has become A^5A^5BA in the folk-tradition, perhaps under the influence of the Hungarian–Mari fifth-construction. An AA^5BA variant also exists.[162] The second part also occurs independently as a separate tune. (See Ex. No. 190.)

189 a

É- gő láng-ban fo- rog szi- vem higy- jed é- ret- ted,
Mi- ko- ron e-szem-ben jut-nak be-szél- ge- té- sid,

b

c

Ki- csi ku- tya tar- ka ne u- gass hi- á- ba,
Van ne- kem sze- re- tőm Som- lyó vá- ro- sá- ba,

Gya- kor-ta ve-lem el-köz-lött sok vi- gas-sá- gid,

Nem ad- nám a sző- két szé- les ez vi- lá- gért.

Sze- rel- me- sen or- cám- ra hányt ked- ves csók- ja- id.

De még a bar- nát sem Kis Ma- gyar- or- szágért!

Transylvanian Folksongs: No. 101. Gyergyószentmiklós
(Csík County), 1910. K.

Tempo giusto

190

Ëgy nagy ó- rú bó- ha Ugy ná-lunk ka - pott vót,

E- bé- dën, va-cso- rán Min-dig csak ná - lunk vót.

The more the 'main trunk' of a tune throws out side-shoots in the Hungarian tradition, the more certainly does it belong here.

Gipsies may well have played this tune as a Rumanian dance (although it is more likely that Chován has simply mistaken its derivation). But that it is Hungarian is not open to doubt until enough comparable sung versions with Rumanian texts are shown to exist in the Rumanian folk repertory. So far there is no sign of their presence.

FOREIGN PIECES OF UNKNOWN ORIGIN

Even text is not always reliable evidence of origin. The best-known tune to the *csűrdöngölő* (barn-stamper, a Transylvanian dance) exists with a text, yet its foreign origin is unquestionable. This tune is found in the *Denkmäler der Tonkunst in Österreich* (No. 1)[163] as a piece entitled 'Gavotta styriaca,' among ballet pieces by J. H. Schmelzer (1623–1680) (Ex. No. 191a). It is possible that it is based on a genuine Styrian folksong, as indicated by the yodel-type motif with its descending sixth. (This motif also occurs in the song 'How does the peasant sow?' p. 96, Ex. No. 128.) The tune may have come to Hungary from Vienna by the normal route of international dance music, transmitted by higher ranks of the Hungarian aristocracy or (as Dénes Balásy contends[164]) through German–Austrian soldiers. Peasants have never been heard to sing it. They do indeed dance to the instrumental 'csűrdöngölő,' quoted as Ex. No. 191d, but instead of singing, they only shout 'dance-words' to it. No. 191b (Bartalus, Vol. I, No. 99) s a unique example of instrumental music with text. If the evidence is reliable, it is a rare case where 'dance-words' are *sung* (not shouted) to the tune (as in the example below, 191c).[165]

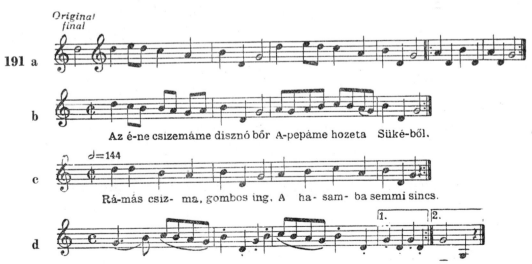

191 a

b

Az é-ne csızemáme disznó bôr A-pepáme hozeta Süké-ből.

c

Rá-más csiz- ma, gombos ing. A ha- sam- ba semmi sincs.

d

The entire tune is instrumental in type; the continuous repetition of pairs of bars shows it to be a primitive dance.

To sum up: in every piece of instrumental music, an unknown, forgotten song may lie concealed, if the four-line structure of our songs is discernible. Other pieces, of origin at present unknown, which stand out as being different in style and construction, may either derive from Western European dance-forms—as in the case of the *csűrdöngölő*—or else show traces of the medieval minstrel tradition.

A few tunes of Bessarabian Turkish (Gagaus) origin point to the existence of close links in this direction.[166]

Primitive traces. Once in possession of the necessary data, it will not be surprising if medieval elements also are shown to have survived in Hungarian folk-dance music. Indeed, there is reason to believe that the primitive, irregularly repeated pairs of bars, often heard on the bagpipe, are remnants of an even remoter past. Hungarian bagpipers always play song tunes, but after a few variations they turn to a figured closing passage, the *aprája* (diminution). This is either without text or else has short improvised dance-words belonging to it. Often interminably repeated, the *aprája* is nothing but primitive dance music consisting of very few notes (= oligotonic); its form is like that of children's songs. It is analogous to the Coda added by gipsy musicians at the end of the *csárdás*, which also consists of short repeated motifs.[167] Here are a few *aprája* motifs. A single motif is repeated at least two or three times, and sometimes as many as eight or ten, before going on to another.

Consisting of 4 bars

192

Consisting of 2 bars

Consisting of 1 bar

Sometimes these motifs are run together for some time without a song tune; almost always slight variations are made on repetition (not shown here):

Only once is there an odd-numbered repetition of the pairs of bars. This may be as accidental as the ¾ bar at the beginning.

More recent art-music influence on the bagpipe. Bagpipers have tried to keep pace with the times as well as faithfully retaining these ancient traces. In illustration, here is a melody from Erkel's national opera *László Hunyadi* (1844), as played by a bagpiper. Naturally he knew nothing of the origin of the piece or of its composer. He believed it to be a German song or a polka dance tune. His scale lacked the sixth, and he tried to compensate for this as best he could by slightly lowering the seventh:

IX FOLK-TRADITION AND MUSICAL CULTURE

An attempt has been made to describe the various strata of the traditional Hungarian song-repertory in terms of style and origin. More recent strata have been superimposed on the original stratum, and this itself cannot be further analysed. These later strata derive from, and relate to, the original stratum, and various foreign elements have also been incorporated.

It must be emphasized that the song-repertory analysed in this book constitutes a single, indivisible whole. It is essentially an expression of life, and instinctively satisfies the musical needs of the peasants. The greater part of the Hungarian nation has so far remained an ethnic community, particularly where music is concerned; it has in common its original folk-culture, which has been preserved intact. Thanks to this, the single song, or flower, of this folk-culture, is often an authentic masterpiece, and as a living product has often enjoyed a separate existence. It is not just the *trésor des humbles,* for it fulfils the most exacting of cultural requirements. It is no primitive product, but an art matured and refined by thousands of years of evolution: an art which is valid and perfect, because the culture that produced it was an organic, balanced unity. Nineteenth-century art-song, on the contrary, was merely the product of a semiculture which, for a large part of the nation, represented a transitional stage only.

Mór Jókai, the great romantic novelist, said that in literature 'our Hungarian Helicon had much to learn from field and meadow.' This applies even more to music, which has even less of a written tradition than literature.

If national classicism means the expression of the national spirit in perfect form, it is clear that classical Hungarian music is only to be found in the few thousand melodies of the folk-tradition. Up to now this melodic wealth represents the most perfect musical expression of the national spirit. More than a folk heritage, it is the property of the whole nation, since it once belonged to the whole people; if Hungary really desires an organic musical culture, the whole nation will have to discover it anew.

Those who try to build up a Hungarian musical tradition without this solid foundation are on the wrong track. There has been much talk of this foundation without a clear understanding of what it means. Hungarians as a whole know little about folk music, and so lack a clear picture of its aesthetic, national and human values. This has nothing to do with its ethnographical importance, which is clearly a scientific matter. In this respect may we hope that the problems inherent in Hungarian folk music will interest international research, since they are the direct result of its unique geographical position and historical development.

Hungarians have not been able to get to know their own folk music, as its real nature has been obscured. In part it still suffers, as it always has, from inadequate or worthless transcriptions, which frighten away anyone anxious to explore further, or, worse still, spread unrecognizably distorted forms. Few people have had the opportunity of hearing folksongs in their original environment, since educated Hungarians are either completely cut off from the peasants or because of their foreign ancestry have never come into contact with the peasantry at all. It is for this reason that they cannot as yet distinguish good from bad in folk music, as they probably can in other branches of folk art. *The shortest road to folk music lies through musical education.*

A general musical consciousness will only be formed in Hungary when the one-fifth minority accepts the musical feeling of the four-fifths majority, still regarded with a certain contempt. If it is not built on this foundation, it will be rootlessly diffused in general world culture, or irretrievably lost in the semiculture of internationalism.

The purpose of the folk-tradition is not confined to providing for the musical life of a people. It is closely connected with life, with the life of everyone. It contains in embryo the shape of a great national musical culture. It depends on the educated classes for its growth and full flowering, but they will only find strength for their task through spiritual unity with the peasants.

This is why musical folk-tradition means far more to Hungarians than to Western-European peoples, who created art-music of a high standard many centuries ago. The folk music of the latter has already been absorbed into art-music, so that the works of great masters already supply that ideal which Hungary can only find in its folk music: the organic continuity of national tradition.

Slowly but inexorably, life itself uproots tradition from among the peasants. To take a stand against this natural historical trend would be vain and useless. It is for educated people to adopt and protect traditions, making them an active part of their lives. How this may be done may best be seen in England and in Russia; many encouraging signs are showing themselves in Hungary, too. Interest in folk music is steadily growing. The best Hungarian singers are beginning to realize that an essentially Hungarian singing-style must be based on the way in which peasants interpret traditional songs, not on an adaptation of foreign singing-styles, be they German or Italian.

144

The forms of tradition may vary, but its essence survives unchanged among the people whose spirit it embodies. It will not be long before the educated class in Hungary is able to restore the folk-tradition they have adopted and shaped into artistic forms: restore it, that is, to the national community, to the people that has become a nation.

APPENDIX

(Being the preface to the Hungarian edition of 1937 with such modifications as have become necessary since then)

This study was written for the series 'Magyarság Néprajza' (Ethnography of the Hungarians), and appeared in the Fourth Volume of the series in 1934. Within the dimensions specified, it was not possible to go into details as deeply as might perhaps have been desirable. In addition to summarizing briefly what is already known, the present study endeavours to point out what is not known, and in the context of this latter intention it will not be superfluous to review the task of folk-music research in the near future.

The task may be divided into two parts: one for the countryside, the other for the library.

In the countryside the task is primarily one of collecting. Although we can scarcely expect to come across any more essentially new material, there is a constant need for greater familiarity with, and for newer and more accurate observations on, existing material, as well as a need to supplement incomplete texts.

Since there is still a tendency for texts to be published stripped of their melodies—see, for example, I. Csanádi and L. Vargyas: *Röpülj páva, röpülj* (Fly Peacock, Fly), 1954 (which contains only 50 songs published in the Notes); Gy. Ortutay: *Magyar népköltészet* (Hungarian Folk Poetry) I–II, 1955; and Gy. Ortutay and Ildikó Kriza: *Magyar népballadák* (Hungarian Folk-Ballads), 1968—it is necessary for us to emphasize that melody and text constitute an indivisible unit, that they are inseparable one from the other. It is precisely the organic link of text and melody that defines the genre of the folksong; neither is a complete work in itself. The notation of texts alone is worthless from an ethnographical standpoint, as is that of melodies alone; but the latter has hardly ever been attempted by anyone.

Many believe it is no longer worth collecting today without a recording machine. A sound recording will indeed reveal, like a magnifying glass, the minute details of a melody that are not even perceptible to the unaided ear; but such a magnified image of every single melody is not necessary for the collector. If an experienced musician with a good ear, has made a thorough study of detailed notations, prepared with the aid of sound recordings, he will be able to notate flawlessly in the field, even without a recording device. Particularly in the initial, exploratory phase of collection, it is not worth risking the expense of making good quality recordings.

Since the introduction of the more efficient gramophone and tape recorder into folk-music research, the chief task of the researcher roaming the countryside has become the selection of the most suitable persons for studio recordings. This too cannot take place without preliminary and thorough collecting work. The procedure most to be deprecated is that of recording a song that

I

146

has not previously been written down in notation. The subsequent notation of such melodies presents great difficulties, not only when this is done from old phonograph cylinders, but even when done from tapes and discs. The texts of these are often unintelligible.

But there are other things to be done in the field for which no recording machine is needed. One of these is the observation of tempo. It is not possible to determine the authentic tempo of a song on the basis of one or two recordings only. The tempo of a recording is often quite different from that in life. We must hear a melody many times, on different occasions, with a metronome at hand, before we can distinguish the customary from the exceptional tempo. We can only obtain a sense of tempo changes within a melody, and their constant, typical or exceptional character, on the basis of many times repeated, on-the-spot observations. Even should folk-music research receive unexpectedly abundant financial support, it is inconceivable that there would ever be as many recordings as are needed for the observation of a single song.

Then there is an aspect of music in the observation of which the phonograph, in fact, sometimes even modern sound-recording not only does not help, but misleads. This is timbre and accent. It alters timbre, sometimes it does not record accent, sometimes it creates an accent where none exists. The ear is more sensitive to both than the recording apparatus. Their ultimate fire details can only be determined by direct listening.

No recording device is required to examine the relationship between text and melody, but for better clarification of this aspect we still require a great amount of data. Which texts are constantly associated, which are more loosely linked, which change their tunes? An individual change of melody, if not confirmed by the community, may be the result of a chance error. It is also necessary to hear melodies with several stanzas again and again, sung in groups and individually. How does the rhythm of the melody change from stanza to stanza? Does it change when accompanied by the same text, or does it remain unchanged with different texts?

The mere notation of a text and melody, however accurate, tells us nothing yet of the life—the physiology—of the melody. We must determine whether it changes on repetition, or in time from the lips of the same singer? Is change intentional or involuntary? Does further spread always represent a change, or not? What are the circumstances, the causes, and the regular features of change? On the basis of data on places and persons written down long ago, it is possible to track down former singers once again. We may be certain of making observations of great interest: has the performance of the songs changed, or not, in the course of years and decades? If the singers are no longer alive, has any trace of the song remained, or did it vanish with them? Have musical tastes changed with the change in living conditions? Why have they ceased to sing certain songs?

An object of separate study is the role of music in the life of the community. How much is it esteemed, and how important is it to the community? How great is the need for music? Does the community appreciate an outstanding singing talent, or does it regard singing with disfavour and regard it as an idle pastime? Does it only regard as a 'good singer' someone who attracts attention by performing a few 'elegant' songs, not in general use in the community, in an affected manner? To what extent does the socially leading stratum aspire 'upwards' even in its musica tastes? Does this influence the rest of the community? Does the ever more sharply differentiated village proletariat separate itself from the small-holding class in musical taste also? Do they still have songs in common? Which songs are linked with class?

We know little about the prevalence of melodies. How deeply rooted are they in the society? How many people know them; can they be defined within some narrower circle? What is the nature of singing occasions, of singing customs? What is the mode of propagation: by hearing only, or with the help of writing or printing? (Written, printed song-books at the fair.) Does conscious, deliberate learning of songs exist, or do new tunes happen to 'stick' with whoever hears them? How important a role is played by the melody, or by the text, in propagation? Are texts without melodies known, and conversely? Are new texts consciously fitted to old melodies? Does someone undertake to compose them?

We have still no exact knowledge of folk-singing technique, vocal range, aural acuity or musical comprehension. How large is the average song-repertory, where does exceptional memory begin, does it always go hand-in-hand with exceptional performing ability? Nor do we have sufficient knowledge of folk-musical instruments and their use. How does the player learn his instrument, by himself, or from someone else? When and what does he play, and for whom? Does he play for money, for dancing, or just for amusement? No accurate data on peasant bands, or on the musical life of the musically illiterate village gipsies are available. What kind of instruments do they use, who organizes them, who teaches them, how do they prepare—individually and in ensemble—for performance? How do they increase their repertory?

No recording machine is needed for the investigation of any of the foregoing problems, yet many of them have remained unstudied so far. Moreover, valuable work in musical folklore can be accomplished without writing down a single melody. It would be particularly informative, for example, if a comprehensive melodic map of some community were prepared, together with a description, giving every detail of its musical life—in a word, a monograph, either as a musical monograph or as an integral part of a general ethnographical description of a single village.

Since the first publication of this last suggestion, monographs have been prepared on the music of three villages: Lajos Vargyas has written a study of the community of Áj, Pál Járdányi of Kide, and István Halmos of Kérsemjén.[168] Their results should inspire others to embark on similar ventures.

Work in the countryside requires prolonged residence in the same place, constant contact with the same people. The itinerant collector played a useful role in the past, when he could obtain a wealth of material within a short time, and there are certain collectors of curiosities who still strive to visit as many places as they can. But answers to our most important questions are to be expected primarily from investigations based on prolonged observation of a given locality.

II   Those who lack the desire or aptitude to work in the countryside may yet serve the cause of research in the library. Here, too, someone who is himself a collector and familiar with the folk heritage from the living material, and not merely from paper, will be at an advantage. Anyone in whom the complete picture of living folksong, built up from auditory images, does not exist, will feel this lack time and again. Purely textual research is most likely to be able to do without it. We do not question its justification and would emphasize that there is an abundance of tasks for literary historical studies, following the pioneering initiative of János Horváth. As yet no attempt at systematic research into the connections between folksong texts and our past literature has been made. A critique of the style of folk poetry cannot rest on a sound basis without such an attempt. Nor have we as yet compared our texts with those of neighbouring peoples.

The musicological aspect of library work comprises research into the origin of the melodies and their interrelations, partly through the folklore material of other peoples, and partly through what has come down to us from musical history. In both these areas the faultless publication of material is still rare. First, it is desirable that a systematic and complete publication of the Hungarian song-repertory should be at the disposal of the researcher. Secondly, a comprehensive study of the relics of Hungarian musical history is necessary. The fact that the sources available today have still not been exhausted is revealed by the few examples of this kind of study as are at present available.

We have still to await collections of scientific value from those related Eastern peoples who most interest us, though one or two gratifying contributions from these sources have already occurred. (See the list at the end of Note No. 18.) This could also be a task for Hungarian scholarship. In the absence of world wars it will undoubtedly come closer to realization, and it would be lacking in confidence to remove it for ever from the list of aims of Hungarian scientific research. Recent Soviet–Hungarian cooperation has made it possible for László Vikár, in collaboration with the linguist Gábor Bereczky, to make several collecting tours among related peoples living in the Volga region. (A list of their results is also given at the end of Note No. 18.)

To this extent, folk music is of significance for ethnographical science. But it has grown far beyond the limits of science. In the life of a healthy nation it is an omnipresent integral part: it penetrates into the arts, into public education, and into the manifestations of social life. Wherever and whenever folk music is relegated to the background, this is a sign of degeneration in national life.

We are far from enjoying the degree of fullness in national culture enjoyed by the great peoples of Europe, and it is for this reason that folk music is not so much within the public consciousness, within the bloodstream of the whole nation in our country as it is, for example, in England. Lately it has seemed as if interest in it were increasing. This indeed was what prompted me to devote time and energy to such a study, even though the time is not yet ripe for a definitive summary. If then I have been unable to offer a complete and rounded work, may it yet serve as a prelude to that further research which in turn will pave the way to a finer, fuller life for Hungarian music.

Zoltán Kodály

NOTES

The phonograph records of the Hungarian Ethnographical Museum are referred to as Ph. E. M., the tape recordings (transferred to gramophone discs) are in the custody of the 'Folk Music Research Group' of the Hungarian Academy of Sciences (referred to as AP).

Block letters indicate tune-construction, ABCD is a 4-line tune in which no two lines are exactly alike. AA^5BA is the commonly known (new-style) Hungarian folksong form: the second line repeats the first a fifth higher, the fourth is the same as the first. ABBA is the form that occurs most frequently in the new-style Hungarian folksong repertory. The Hungarian–Mari fifth construction is A^5A^5AA and A^5B^5AB.

The tunes have all been reduced to a common final, so that the fourth line always ends on g_1. For the sake of brevity, the last notes of the other lines are given as numbers in various kinds of frames.

195

The three signs $\boxed{1}\ \boxed{\flat 3}\ \boxed{5}$ indicate, for example, a tune in which the first line ends on g_1, the second on b_1 flat and the third on d_2. If the fourth line has an irregular final, it is indicated by a double frame. The *sol-fa* letters are given in relation to the *do*; in major tunes, the tonic *(do)* is *g*, in minor and pentatonic tunes it is *b* flat.

1 See Chapter VIII, p. 133.

2 With reference to Hungarian musical culture and musical literacy in the Middle Ages see: *Deákság és Európa* [The Hungarian 'Clericus' and Europe] by László Mezey, in press. (Ch. I, This footnote refers to p. 13. of the present work.)

3 The first investigations of this kind were made by György Kerényi in *Magyar népdalok és népies dalok* [Hungarian Folksongs and Popular Art-Songs]. Budapest, 1961, Vol. III; *Népies dalok* [Popular Art-Songs], compiled by György Kerényi; and lastly: *Szentirmay Elemér* by György Kerényi, Budapest, 1965. (Ch. I, p. 15.)

4 J. Horváth: *A magyar irodalmi népiesség Faluditól Petőfiig* [The Folk Element in Hungarian Literature from Faludi to Petőfi]. Budapest, 1927. (Ch. I, p. 15.)

150

5 *A Kisfaludy Társaság népköltési gyűjteménye* [The Kisfaludy Society's Collection of Folk Poetry]. I–XIV, 1872–1924. László Arany, son of the poet János Arany, was himself a poet and an expert on folk poetry and folk-tradition. Gyulai was at this time a critic and connoisseur of importance. (Ch. I, p. 15.)

6 Published, critically revised by D. Bartha and J. Kiss, 1953. — The 1813 MS. and the MS. of István Tóth (1832–43) both belong to the Library of the Hungarian Academy of Sciences. The MS. of 1814 appears to have been lost. (Ch. I, p. 16.)

7 'Mon intention était... de m'enfoncer seul, à pied, le sac sur le dos, dans les parties les plus désertes de la Hongrie. Il n'en fut point ainsi.' The original French text was not published until 1912 with the title *Pages Romantiques* (Éditions Chantavoinc, Paris: Alcan, p. 235). German translation: F. Liszt, *Gesammelte Schriften*, Vol. II, p. 225, Leipzig, Breitkopf und Härtel. (Ch. I, p. 16.)

8 J. Horváth, *op. cit.*, Note No. 4; *Kazinczy levelezése* [Kazinczy's Correspondence]. Vol. III, p. 112. (Ch. I, p. 16.)

9 *Magyar népdalok (énekre és zongorára) vagy egyedül (zongorára) alkalmazák (Fogarasi és Travnyik), a Kisfaludy-Társaság megbízásábul kiadja Erdélyi János* [Hungarian Folksongs Arranged for Voice and Pianoforte, or for Pianoforte alone, by Fogarasi and Travnyik. Published under the auspices of the Kisfaludy Society by János Erdélyi]; appeared in Pest in 1847 in two (undated) volumes. Another collection with a similar title appeared in 1846 in Vienna, according to S. E. Major; sec *Ethnographia*, 1939, pp. 316 and 319. The only known copy was lost in the Second World War. In his preface to *Magyar népdalok és mondák* [Hungarian Folksongs and Legends] Erdélyi lists all the manuscript music received from various collectors. These manuscripts seem to have disappeared, and so far only two have since come to light. See the author's study 'Magyar zenei folklore száztíz év előtt' [Hungarian Musical Folklore 110 Years Ago]. *Magyarságtudomány*, Vol. II, 1943, and reprint. This also contains further information on Mindszenty and Udvardy. (Ch. I, p. 17. See also CMPH Vol. I, p. X.)

10 Here are a few details of the number of purely pentatonic tunes to be found in older collections. Those of Ádám Pálóczi-Horváth and István Tóth each contain a single example out of totals of 366 and 318, respectively. In that of István Bartalus, 4 out of 730 tunes are purely pentatonic (one has four variants), and 18 are recognizable. G. Mátray's collection contains not one pure example, and only 4 out of 93 are recognizably pentatonic. Even these few went unnoticed. The pentatonic stratum of Hungarian folk music was revealed only by modern collectors. See the author's 'Ötfokú hangsor a magyar népzenében' [Pentatonic Scale in Hungarian Folk Music]. *Zenei Szemle*, 1917, reprinted with several additions in the *Memorial Volume* (1929) of the Sepsiszentgyörgy Museum; and his *Visszatekintés* [In Retrospect]. Collected writings, addresses and statements, Vol. II, p. 57. (Ch. I, p. 18.)

11 Gyula Szekfű: 'A magyarság és a faji kérdés' [Hungarians and the Racial Question] in *Történetpolitikai tanulmányok*, Budapest, 1924. (Ch. I, p. 18.)

12 Sentimental Italianate songs became quite as popular as folksongs among the Russian nobility, in just the same way. As for the Rumanian middle class, see Bartók: *A magyar népdal* [Hungarian Folk Music], footnote 1, p. 56 in English edition (Oxford University Press,

1931). (German edition, p. LXIX, Berlin–Leipzig, 1925, W. de Gruyter und Co.). As the cultural level rises, middle and upper classes tend universally to forsake national and folk-traditions, and to succumb to styles of foreign culture. Eighteenth-century German princes cultivated French literature and Italian opera: for a long time this latter held even the French and English—in cultural matters the most self-sufficient of nations—in its sway. (Ch. I, p. 19.)

13 János Horváth, *op. cit.*, p. 11. (Ch. I, p. 19.)

14 See Paul Levy: 'Geschichte des Begriffes Volkslied.' *Acta Germanica* VII (1911); Julian Pulikowski: *Geschichte des Volkslied-Begriffes im musikalischen Schrifttum: ein Stück deutscher Geistesgeschichte.* Heidelberg, 1933. (Ch. I, p. 20.)

15 A small section of the collection was also published. Páter Domokos Pál–Benjamin Rajeczky: *Csángó népzene* [Csángó Folk Music]. I–II, Budapest, 1956, 1961; József Faragó–János Jagamas: *Moldvai csángó népdalok és népballadák* [Moldavian Csángó Folksongs and Folk-Ballads]. Bucharest, 1954; Zoltán Kallós: 'Ismeretlen balladák Moldvából' [Unknown Ballads from Moldavia]. *Néprajzi Közlemények* III/1–2 (1958), pp. 51–70; *Somogyi táncok* [Dances of Somogy]. Compiled by Péter Morvay and Ernő Pesovár. Budapest, 1954. (Ch. I, p. 20.)

16 Closer study may soon produce results here, too. It is not known with any certainty how individual examples of new-style Hungarian folksong-types reached the Finnish repertory; it may have been through literary transmission. See, for instance, 'Suomen Kansan Sävelmiä.' *Laulusävelmiä*, Vol. III, 1921, 1937, No. 2070. The relationship of several Kalevala tunes to a Hungarian song-type, of which the following may serve as an example,

Somogyszob (Somogy County). L. V.

196

Poco rubato ♩ = 63

Is-ten hozzád szülöt - tem föld. Én mi-attam le-hetsz már zöld.

Ti - por-ta - lak, nem ti - por - lak, Is-ten hozzád, már itt - hagy - lak.

was pointed out many years ago by the author (*Nyelvtudományi Közlöny*, 1906, p. 131). It is not known for certain whether such parallels indicate an ancient relationship between the two. Nevertheless, the Transylvanian 'regös' song (Transylvanian Folksongs, No. 1, in the present work p. 135, Ex. No. 184) is closely related to a common Finnish type (*Laulusävelmiä*, Nos. 3301, 3304 ff.). Judging by these analogies it would seem to be a half-tune. It occurs as such in Finnish material, *loc. cit.*, 3204 ff., and in many other places. For the 4-line form, see *Ethnographia*, 1947, pp. 296–298. Hungarian–Finnish melodic comparisons are contained in the following works: György Szomjas-Schiffert: *Finnisch-ugrische Herkunft der ungarischen 'Regös'-Gesänge.* Congressus Internationalis Fenno-Ugristarum Budapestini Habitus 1960. 1963, pp. 364–396. The same author: 'Die finnisch-ugrische Abstammung der ungarischen Regös-Gesänge und der Kalevala-Melodien.' *Musik des Ostens*, Kassel-

Basel, 1963, pp. 126–156. The same author: *A finnugorság ősi zenéje nyomában. Összehasonlító módszertan* [Tracing the Ancient Music of the Finno-Ugrians. A Comparative Method]. Reprint: *Magvető Almanach*, 1965/3, pp. 1–64. The same author: 'Les traditions communes des peuples finno-ougriens dans leurs mélodies de danse.' *Études Finno-Ougriennes*, 1966, pp. 105–123. The same author: *Der Kalevala-Typ in den gemeinsamen Melodien der finno-ugrischen Völker.* Congressus Secundus Internationalis Fenno-Ugristarum, Helsinki, 1965. Pars II, pp. 310–324. The same author: 'Kalevala, regösének, "páva-dallam" ' [The Kalevala, the Year Greeting Song, the 'Peacock Song']. *Ethnographia*, 1967, pp. 452–465. Béla C. Nagy: 'Adatok a magyar népdal kialakulásához' [Data on the Development of the Hungarian Folksong]. *Zenetudományi Tanulmányok*, 1959, pp. 605–688. The same author: 'A magyar népdal eredete' [The Origin of Hungarian Folksong]. *Zenei Szemle*, 1947, pp. 203–213. The same author: 'A siratódallam' [The Lament]. *Ethnographia*, 1961, pp. 385–401. The same author: 'Typenprobleme in der ungarischen Volksmusik.' *Studia Musicologica*, 1962. For a Finno-Ugric comparison see Lajos Vargyas: *Zur Methodik der vergleichenden finnisch-ugrischen Musikwissenschaft.* Congressus Secundus Internationalis Fenno-Ugristarum. Helsinki, 1965, Pars II, pp. 377–382. (Ch. II, p. 23.)

17 This same phenomenon is described by Cecil J. Sharp in *English Folksongs from the Southern Appalachians.* Ed. by Maud Karpeles, London–New York–Toronto, 1952, in the introduction, and in the notes to the songs 5B, 49M, 82F, G and 106D; as well as in *English Folksongs: Some Conclusions.* 3rd ed. rev. by Maud Karpeles, London, 1954, p. 71. Bartók observed it in Cheremis phonograph cylinders of the Ethnographical Museum, and in Rumanian and Serbian folksongs, also. The neutral third also exists in the traditional tuning of the Caucasian pan pipes. For comparisons see Lajos Vargyas: 'Some Parallels of Rare Modal Structures in Western and Eastern Europe.' *Journal of the International Folk Music Council*, 1958, pp. 23–24. (Ch. II, p. 25.)

18 The Cheremis (Mari) examples are taken from the following sources: *Sammelbände der Internationalen Musikgesellschaft* (SIMG) III, 1902–1903, pp. 430 and 741 ff., where 15 tunes are quoted by Ilmari Krohn. Mrs. Yrjö Wichmann's gramophone records in the Ethnographic Section of the Hungarian National Museum were transcribed by Béla Bartók (24 tunes). V. W. Vasiliev: *Mari Muro* (Kazan, 1920), 304 tunes; a second similar collection (Moscow, 1923), 167 tunes, and a third collection (Moscow, 1937), 221 tunes. This last is known thanks to the zeal of Kató Vargyas who, during her stay in Moscow, copied down the tunes of several unobtainable collections. I. S. Klutchnikov: *Marla Murash Tunekteso Savesh* (Moscow, 1923), 42 tunes. R. Lach: *Gesänge russischer Kriegsgefangener*, Vol. I, Part 3. 'Tscheremissische Gesänge.' Vienna, 1929. (Ak. d. Wissenschaften Phil.-Hist. Klasse, Sitzungsberichte 204, Vol. 5 containing 233 tunes, of which roughly 70 are mere variants.) Lach's further publications also appeared in the Vienna Academy edition (*Vorläufiger Bericht*, etc., 1918; *Wotjakische, syrjänische und permiakische Gesänge*, 1926; *Mordwinische Gesänge*, 1933; *Tschuwaschische Gesänge*, 1940). The first gramophone collection of Mari folksongs was published in 1951 in Leningrad and Moscow (*Mari Kalyk Muro;* with comprehensive bibliography). Newer collections: K. Smirnov: *Evrel mari Muro.* Ioskar-Ola, 1951, 100 tunes. — K. Smirnov: *Olik mari Muro.* Ioskar-Ola, 1955, 120 tunes. — I. Espay -

V. Belyayev: *Mari Kalyk Muro*. Moscow, 1957, 80 tunes. – A. R. Sidushkina: *Kirik mari halik mirivle*. Ioskar-Ola, 1958. 53 tunes. — László Vikár collected 1958–1968 on the spot, 856 Cheremis, 422 Chuvash, 131 Tartar, 112 Wotyak and 29 Mordvinian tunes, in collaboration with the linguist, Gábor Bereczky. The recordings may be found in the archives of the 'Folk Music Research Group' of the Hungarian Academy of Sciences. The Phonogram-Archive of the Pushkin House in Leningrad has some 120 tunes. (Ch. II, p. 26.)

19 This is more fully treated in the author's study 'Sajátságos dallamszerkezet a cseremisz népzenében'| [Characteristic Tune-Construction in Mari Folk Music]. *Balassa Memorial Volume*, Budapest, 1934, and reprint, 1935. (Ch. II, p. 26.)

20 Compare also Bartók *Hungarian Folk Music* (No. II on p. 87). Further example, No. 261 and *ibid.*, No. III, p. 87. The completion of the Mari tune quoted in the text is justified by the nine variants of the complete form. Vasiliev, 1923, Nos. 89, 123, 157; SIMG III, p. 741, No. 4, p. 743, No. 25. Lach: *Cheremis Songs*, Nos. 206, 219, and 229. Bartók, *op. cit.*, No, II, p. 87. Half-tunes: Vasiliev, 1923, Nos. 111, 160. Hungarian tunes of similar construction: Bartók and Kodály, *20 Magyar népdal* [20 Hungarian Folksongs]. 1906, No. 17. Bartalus, *Folksongs* II, No. 10. (Ch. II, p. 29.)

21 Further variants of this song, recently discovered, reveal how widespread this type is among other peoples as well. See B. Szabolcsi's reconstruction in *Magyar Évkönyv* [Hungarian Year-Book], Vol. XVIII (1938), p. 204. Here are three other forms for comparison with the Hungarian and Mari versions: (a) Chuvash (Maximov: *Turi Dovassen Jurissem*. Piesni Verkhovikh Chuvash. Shupashkar, 1932, No. 161). In the original, the first half of the tune is an octave lower. It is in 4/4 time, with two up-beat crotchets; (b) Kalmuc (Rudnev: *Melodii Mongolskikh plemen*. St. Petersburg, 1909, No. 58, with the original up-beat of the second tune-line); (c) Mongolian (Bashkuyev: *Zbornik Buryat-Mongolskikh pesen*. Moscow, 1935, No. 31):

B. Szabolcsi, in his *A melódia története* [History of Melody], 1950, p. 130, 1957,[2] p. 297
(German version: *Bausteine zu einer Geschichte der Melodie*, 1959, p. 261), adds a further
Chinese parallel:

198

Lack of comparative material still makes it impossible to define the area in which this tune-
structure commonly occurs. Recently discovered Chinese collections reveal—and promise
yet more—surprising similarities to Hungarian–Mari–Chuvash tune-types. The finals of the
Chinese examples are interchangeably *g* and *f*. Examples from *Hopei min chien ko ch'ü
hsüan* [Selected Folksongs from Hopei]. Shanghai, 1953:

199

(Ch. II, p. 32.)

22 Apart from those mentioned, see also: Bartók: *Hungarian Folk Music*, Nos. 302, 201, 261,
21, 40, 67, 71a, 72, 74a. Traces of this kind *ibid.*, Nos. 6, 8, 15, 18, 20, 22, 24–27, 29–36,
38, 39, 41–45, 48, 49, 51, 53, 54a and b, 56–58, 65, 74b, 167, 259d. *Transylvanian Folksongs*, Nos. 135, 140, 145; major *ibid.*, Nos. 139, 144, 147. Traces of this kind *ibid.*, Nos. 8,
9, 17, 25, 49, 77, 82, 100–103, 111, 113, 123, 134, 141, 146. (Ch. II, p. 35.)

23 Compare the two opening lines of the Hungarian tune with the beginning of the 135th
Geneva psalm. A variant is given by V. M. Vasiliev, 1920, No. 304. (Ch. II, p. 42.)

24 V. A. Moskov: 'Melodii Astrakhanskikh i Orenburgskikh Nogaitsev i Kirgiz.' *Izvestia
Obshchestva Arkheologii, Istorii i Etnografii*, XVII, Kazan, 1901, No. 1. (Ch. II, p. 54.)

25 J. Fogarasi: *Művelt magyar nyelvtan* [The Grammar of Literary Hungarian]. 1843, p. 387:
'But you, who are dedicated to the art of music, look rather for the spirit of Hungarian
music in simple folksongs, and not in these recent and artificial compositions, which are
anything but Hungarian. I speak to those of you who are gifted, for the incompetent cannot
even write down correctly the beautiful and original songs they have heard.' He adds examples in a musical appendix. That his complaint is still valid today is clearly shown by a glance
at Dávid Popper's *Ungarische Rhapsodie*, op. 68, where the widely-known song 'Káka
tövén költ a ruca' [The duck broods in the bulrushes] is given the following rhythm: (Ex.
No. 200). The accented notes of the original are wrongly shown either as (1) unaccented
passing notes or (2) appoggiature. There are similar errors in the other tunes he quotes, even
though Popper spent the greater part of his life in Budaepst! (Ch. II, p. 54.)

26 Jewish variants of this tune-type often occur in the well-known collection *Hebräisch-Orienta-lischer Melodienschatz* of Idelsohn, e.g., 'Gesänge der jemenischen Juden,' Leipzig, 1914, pp. 79, 93, etc., 'Gesänge der babylonischen Juden,' Berlin, 1922, pp. 84, 107, etc. (Ch. II, p. 57.)

27 Further examples: Lach: *Wotjakische, syrjänische und permiakische Gesänge.* 1926, Nos. 3, 5–7, 49, 71. (Ch. II, p. 58.)

28 In Hungarian material, even children's tunes of the same type have a fixed number of syllables. The lament is the only example of recited prose in Hungary. (Ch. II, p. 60.)

29 B. Szabolcsi: 'Eastern Relations of Early Hungarian Folk Music.' *Journal of the Royal Asiatic Society*, 1935; in detail, see *Ethnographia*, 1934, p. 138. (Ch. II, p. 61.)

30 A. O. Väisänen: *Wogulische und ostjakische Melodien* (Helsinki, 1937), a work of great importance, which materially increased our knowledge of the music of the Ob-Ugrians. The material so far available, however, seems insufficient to justify the statements made in his *Untersuchungen über die Obugrischen Melodien* (Helsinki, 1939), which were intended to be definitive. In Hungary, studies by Bence Szabolcsi and Lajos Vargyas seek to demonstrate Ugrian elements in the Hungarian heritage; see Note No. 74. See also the works listed in Note No. 16. (Ch. II, p. 61.)

31 See Bartók: *Hungarian Folk Music*, p. 39. (Ch. III, p. 62.)

32 The form ABBA also occurs in French fifteenth-century popular songs; in Paris-Gevaert's *Chansons du XVe siècle*, 7 out of 142 have this form, in Th. Gérold's *Chansons populaires du XVe–XVIe siècle,* there are 4 out of a total of 50. But in most of these tunes, the A line is a refrain; appearing at the outset, it makes the form appear as ABBA. The continuous form of the melody is ABBABBA. The medieval *Virelai* is similar in form. Compare P. Gennrich: *Grundriss einer Formenlehre des mittelalterlichen Liedes.* Halle, 1932, p. 70ff. Its form, ABBAA, differs from the Hungarian only in the repeating last line. Whether such Western European forms had, or could have had, an influence on the development of Hungarian forms is as yet unanswerable. Nobody has yet made an exhaustive historical analysis of these dominant patterns of Western European music. (Ch. III, p. 63.)

33 See R. von Liliencron: *Deutsches Leben im Volkslied um 1530*, p. 217; Paris-Gevaert: *Chansons du XVe siècle*, 3 examples out of 142. There are 12 examples of ABCA in this work. P. Wagner: *Einführung in die Gregorianischen Melodien*, Vol. III, p. 473, mentions three examples of ABCA and only one of AABA. Benjamin Rajeczky: *Melodiarium Hungariae Medii Aevi*, Vol. I. *Himnuszok és sequentiák* [Hymns and Sequences], 1954, contains 14 ABCA and 4 AABA forms (from 199). Further examples of AABA will be found in Bruno Stäblein's *Monumenta monodica Medii Aevi*, Vol. I, *Hymnen* (I), Kassel–Basel, 1956, Nos. 130$_2$, 702, 22$_6$, 11$_2$, 22$_2$, 11$_1$, etc. (Ch. III, p. 63.)

34 Gennrich, *op. cit.* (see Note No. 32), p. 233, considers that the AABA form of Gregorian hymns is of Syrian origin, quoting Dom Jeannin: *Mélodies liturgiques syriennes et chaldéennes.* Paris, 1925–26. (Ch. III, p. 63.)

35 Paris-Gevaert: *Chansons du XVe siècle*, No. 67. It is related to a 5-line tune-type AA^{5}A^{5}A^{8}A, to be found on p. 13 of the *Locheimer Liederbuch* of *c.* 1450. This melody was taken over by the Church, and appears in sixteenth-century German and Czech hymnbooks. See *Pisny Evangelistskych*, etc., 1576, p. 155 (variant No. 589), and, with the omission of the first line, p. 396. Zahn: *Die Melodien der deutschen evangelischen Kirchenlieder*, No. 4068, 1390. A descendant of this French *chanson* is recognizable in a Hungarian hymn (see Harmat–Sík: 'Szent vagy Uram!' [Holy Art Thou, O Lord!], No. 176.) (Ch. III. p. 63.) |

36 Given by Dénes Bartha with two variants in *A XVIII. század magyar dallamai* [Hungarian 18th-Century Melodies]. Budapest, 1935, No. 121. Of the 215 tunes in this collection, 21 belong to the AABA type, the AA^{5}BA type is represented only by No. 121. (Ch. III, p. 63.)

37 Beethoven's source is most probably Fr. Reichardt: *Frohe Lieder für deutsche Männer.* Berlin, 1781. See Erk-Böhme: *Deutscher Liederhort.* I, Nos. 80, 281. The fourth line of the Hungarian tune is closer to a sixteenth-century German variant, *loc. cit.*, No. 109a. The differences are as follows: In the Hungarian, the up-beat has disappeared, and in the third line it has suffered an interesting displacement. The Hungarian first line is the same as the German fourth line. The German second line does not go up to a_2, only to g_a. This is the 'tonal answer' familiar in Western music and frequent in fifteenth and sixteenth-century tunes. It also exists in Hungarian folk music. See, for example, Bartók: *Hungarian Folk Music*, Nos. 87, 88, 102, 110, 113, 124, 277, 295a. Regarding its further prevalence in Europe see Walter Wiora: *Europäischer Volksgesang.* Köln, n. d., No. 70. (Ch. III. p. 65.)

38 For this, see Bartók: *Hungarian Folk Music*, p. 50. For the Mari material, see the author's work mentioned in Note No. 19. The original fifth-construction of many Hungarian folk tunes may have been obscured by the high opening line having dropped an octave. If, for example, the first line of No. 26 or 66 (in Bartók's book) is raised an octave, some trace of the answer at the lower fifth at once appears in the third tune-line. (Ch. III, p. 68.)

39 J. Horváth: *A középkori magyar vers ritmusa* [The Rhythm of Medieval Hungarian Verse]. 1928, p. 66. A characteristic instance is the hymn 'Salve, mater misericordiae.' This rhythm may also have reached the peasantry through a few widely-known hymns, 'Angyaloknak nagyságos asszonya' [Gracious Lady of the Angels], 'Felvitetett magas mennyországba' [Raised to High Heaven], etc. It is doubtful, however, whether the peasants heard accurate versions of their original rhythms. (See *Cantus Catholici*, 1651. A new edition in Vajthó's *Irodalmi ritkaságok* [Literary Rarities], Nos. 35, 38, 39.) (Ch. III, p. 70.)

40 Bartók: *Hungarian Folk Music*, No. 58. In other respects also this tune shows a definite kinship with a new style song, No. 105 in Bartók's book. (Ch. III, p. 70.)

41 Bartók, *op. cit.*, Nos. 122, 130. Dorian: *ibid.*, No. 90, and also Nos. 102, 117, 138, 147. Aeolian: *ibid.*, Nos. 124 and 126. The pentatonic structure may be concealed beneath a Mixolydian exterior, just as the old pentatonic form has been transformed into Mixolydian. See Bartók, *op. cit.*, Nos. 9, 33c. See the following examples:

Bartók, No. 113. Vésztő (Békés County), 1906. B.

201

Tempo giusto ♩ = 116

Túl a Tiszán juhászlegény vagyok én.   Harminchárom birkára vi - gyázok én.

Gyere babám, téritsd meg a birka e - le - jét.   Ne jegye le a bodorka le - ve - lét!

Bartók, No. 102. Vésztő (Békés County), 1906. B.

202

Tempo giusto ♩ = 88

Ká sát et tem, meg- é get tem a szá mat.

Ki vi se li gond ját az én a nyám nak?

Én már lá tom, nem vi se lem sze - gény nek,

Ol tal má - ra bi zom a jó Is ten nek.

Pátria record No. 49/B. Rimóc (Nógrád County).

203

Tempo giusto

E-sik e-ső, e - sik, szép csëndesën e - sik, ta-vasz a-kar lën ni.

De sze - ret - nék a babám kiskertjébe të - a - ró - zsa lën ni.

Nem le-he-tek én ró - zsa, el - hër-vaszt a ka-to-na-ru - ha.

Buda - pes - ti, három e-me- le-tës tü - zér kaszár nyá - ba.

(Ch. III, p. 70.)

42 Pál Járdányi: *Magyar népdaltípusok* [Hungarian Folksong Types]. Budapest, 1961, Vol. II, pp. 35, 55 and 91 are similar. (Ch. III, p. 71.)

43 Two Hungarian folksongs: I 'Hej! Gazd'uram kérem' [Hey, master, please], II 'Csicsáéknál ég a világ' [A light is burning in the Csicsas' house], from the folk play *A kis gróf szerelme* [The Love of the Little Count], setting by G. Pávay. Rózsavölgyi and Co., No. 648. The version is taken from Mrs. Lóránd Szunyogh's *Nótáskönyv* [Song-Book], which appeared in 1900. There is no essential difference between the two versions. *A kis gróf szerelme* is a play about village life by Kornél Ábrányi, Jr. It was first produced on 10 August, 1877 in the Budapest Folk Theatre, with music by Gyula Erkel. The manuscript is deposited in the Library of the Hungarian National Theatre, but does not include this tune, which may have been added later. (Ch. III, p. 74.)

44 See K. Jeppesen: *Der Palestrinastil und die Dissonanz*. Leipzig, 1925. English: *The Style of Palestrina and the Dissonance*. London, Oxford Univ. Press, 1946. (Ch. III, p. 75.)

45 O. Fleischer: *Ein Kapitel vergleichender Musikwissenschaft* (Sammelbände der I. M. G. Vol. I, 1899). Examples of the complete scale: Áron Kiss: *Magyar gyermekjátékgyűjtemény* [Hungarian Children's Games]. 1891, pp. 147, 148. CMPH Vol. I, Ch. II–VII. (Ch. IV, p. 77.)

46 CMPH Vol. I (Children's Games), 27. The tune can also go down to *re-do*; cf. No. 92 with Nos. 35 and 36. (Ch. IV, p. 77.)

47 *Ibid.* 58. An even closer form is No. 96. (Ch. IV, p. 77.)

48 *Ibid.* 313. Cf. also Nos. 304, 305, 307, 308, 314, 319. (Ch. IV, p. 77.)

49 *Ibid.* 306, 309–312, 315. (Ch. IV, p. 77.)

50 *Ibid.* 237, see also 158–160. (Ch. IV, p. 77.)

51 *Ibid.* 429. Cf. also 161. (Ch. IV, p. 78.)

52 *Ibid.* 122, 1129. This form is related to tunes such as No. 56. (Ch. IV, p. 78).

53 *Ibid.* 58, 502, 513, 602. (Ch. IV, p. 78.)

54 *Ibid.* 60, 73. (Ch. IV, p. 78.)

55 *Ibid.* 943–948. (Ch. IV, p. 78.)

56 *Ibid.* 176. (Ch. IV, p. 78.)

57 *Ibid.* Ch. IX and No. 168. (Ch. IV, p. 78.)

58 *Ibid.* Ch. XVIII. (Ch. IV, p. 78.)

59 *Ibid.* 197, 384. (Ch. IV, p. 78.)

60 *Ibid.* 313. (Ch. IV, p. 78.)

61 *Ibid.* 18–20, 36, 82, 94, 107, 135, 141, 144, 337, 668, 948, etc. (Ch. IV, p. 78.)

62 *Ibid.* 70, 215. (Ch. IV, p. 78.)

63 *Ibid.* 956 ff. (Ch. IV, p. 78.)

64 *Ibid.* Appendix to Ch. IX. (Ch. IV, p. 78.)

65 *Ibid.* 992. (Ch. IV, p. 79.)

66 Á. Kiss, *op. cit.*, p. 444. (Ch. IV, p. 79.)

67 *Ethnographia*, 1901, pp. 145 and 201. (Ch. IV, p. 83.)

68 Giulio Fara: *L'anima musicale d'Italia*. Rome, 1920, p. 198 ff. See in particular the Corsican laments that incited vendettas. (Ch. V, p. 85.)

69 H. Pernot: *Mélodies populaires grecques de l'île de Chio*. Paris, 1903, p. 8: 'On a la plus grande peine à obtenir ces aires funèbres, car ils sont toujours accompagnés de larmes et de douleur réelle.' (Ch. V, p. 85.)

70 A fragment of the text was published in 1872, in the second volume of *Magyar népköltési gyűjtemény* [Collection of Hungarian Folk Poetry], p. 346. Cf. also *ibid.*, p. 496. A fulle description occurs in *Magyarország képekben* [Hungary in Pictures]. 1867, p. 61 ff. A tune from Baranya County is given by *Ethnographia*, 1901, p. 29. Its authenticity is doubtfu, because of its very complexity. For the North Hungarian type from the Zobor region see *Zenei Lexikon* [Musical Lexicon], 1930–1931, Vol. II, p. 67. Data from the Alföld: L. Kiss: *Régi népdalok Hódmezővásárhelyről* [Old Folksongs from Hódmezővásárhely]. 1927, p. 46, written from memory with the text inaccurately set to the music. The same appears without text in *Ethnographia*, 1920, p. 87. Laments from Nagyszalonta published by the author, see *Magyar népköltési gyűjtemény* [Collection of Hungarian Folk Poetry], Vol. XIV, 1924, pp. 298–301. A further forty variants or so had been taken down in notation before we began to compile Volume V of the CMPH. Laments are to be found on records Nos. 25, 43 and 71 of the Hungarian Radio's Gramophone Record Collection (Pátria). A few texts are to be found in G. Kiss's *Ormánság*. Budapest, 1937, p. 121 ff. (Ch. V, p. 85.)

71 The Greek writer Lucian is alone in having recorded the text of a father's lament for his son—albeit in a satirical description. (*De Luctu*, 13.) (Ch. V, p. 85.)

72 The Romans used hired mourners (praeficae); but originally a member of the family sang the lament. The facts are difficult to establish. Some researchers into Transylvanian-Saxon folklore maintain that paid mourning women existed, while others deny this. Böckel: *Psychologie der Volksdichtung*. Leipzig, 1906, p. 105, Note No. 2. G. Kiss, *op. cit.*, Note No. 70. (Ch. V, p. 86.)

73 Other collectors tell of similar experiences. Böckel, *op. cit.*, p. 2; Weigand: *Die Aromunen*. Vol. II, p. 200. (Ch. V. p. 86.)

74 Studies on song-types, both foreign and Hungarian, related to the Hungarian lament, are as follows: Bence Szabolcsi: 'Osztyák hősdalok — magyar siratók melódiái' [Ostyak Epic Songs—Melodies of Hungarian Laments]. *Ethnographia*, 1933, 71, and 'Osztyák és vogu dallamok. Újabb adatok a magyar népi siratódallam problémájához' [Ostyak and Vogul Melodies. Additional Data to the Problem of Hungarian Folk Laments]. *Ethnographia*, 1937, 340, point out Ob-Ugrian parallels between small and large laments with $\boxed{2}$ $\boxed{\boxed{1}}$ or $\boxed{5}$ $\boxed{\boxed{4}}$ and $\overline{5}$ $\boxed{4}$ $\boxed{2}$ $\boxed{\boxed{1}}$ cadences. Lajos Vargyas: 'Ugrische Schicht in der ungarischen Volksmusik'. *Acta Ethnographica*, 1950, 161, and expanded 'Ugor réteg a magyar népzenében' [Ugrian Stratum in Hungarian Folk Music], *Zenetudományi Tanulmányok* I (1953), 611, besides showing further Ugrian parallels between the two types of laments, demonstrates their kinship with numerous strophic types of Hungarian folksong. (Ch. V, p. 89.)

75 Bálint Sárosi: 'Sirató és keserves' [Lament and Complaint]. *Ethnographia*, 1963, pp. 117–122. For the relationship between other types of laments and folksong types see Lajos Vargyas: 'Totenklage und Vorgeschichte der Ungarn' in *Festschrift für Walter Wiora zum 30. Dezember 1966*, 1967, pp. 623–627. For the relationship of our mourning songs to Western styles see

Benjamin Rajeczky: 'Ost und West in den ungarischen Klageliedern' (same source), pp. 628–632. (Ch. V, p. 93.)

76 *A Kisfaludy-Társaság népköltési gyűjteménye*, Vol. XIV, p. 292. (Ch. V, p. 93.)

77 L. Lajtha has published a collection of wake-songs: *Sopron megyei régi magyar virrasztó-énekek* [Old Hungarian Wake-Songs from Sopron County]. Budapest, 1956. (Ch. V, p. 94.)

78 *Népzenénk és a szomszéd népek népzenéje* [Our Folk Music and The Folk Music of Neighbouring Peoples]. Budapest, 1934; *Ungarische Jahrbücher*, Berlin, 1935, and as an off-print in the *Hungarian Library*. Also in French, Rumanian and Slovak. (Ch. VI, p. 95.)

79 János Arany's manuscript song-collection offers a fair number of examples. Published in Budapest, 1952 by Zoltán Kodály–Ágost Gyulai. (Ch. VI, p. 95.)

80 In his poem 'Tamburás öregúr' [The Old Zither Player]. (Ch. VI, p. 95.)

81 Further correspondences are exhibited by melodies of French parlour-game-style dances, originating in the Middle Ages. On the basis of the material known so far, the Hungarian texts resemble the French more closely: the melodies, the German. (Ch. VI, p. 96.)

82 The melody spread, along with the text of the ballad, through cheap publications after 1790, as established by Child. Compare Lajos Vargyas: 'Zur Verbreitung deutscher Balladen und Erzähllieder in Ungarn.' *Festschrift zum 75. Geburtstag von Erich Seemann. Jahrbuch für Volksliedforschung* IX (1964), p. 63. (Ch. VI, p. 96.)

83 Á. P.-Horváth's song-collection, No. 126 and Bartalus: *Magyar Orpheus* [Hungarian Orpheus], p. 5. Peasants still sing it in Transdanubia. In German see, for example, Böhme: *Deutsches Kinderlied*, p. 567, No. 381; p. 662, p. 666, No. 610. Imre Krámer: *A magyarországi német népdal* [German Folksong in Hungary]. Budapest, 1933, p. 64. CMPH Vol. I, pp. 1085–87. (Ch. VI, p. 97.)

84 Bartók: *Hungarian Folk Music*, Nos. 160, 178, 185, 205, 239, 254, 318, also perhaps No. 206. (Ch. VI, p. 98.)

85 Bartók: *Hungarian Folk Music*, p. 73; *Népzenénk* (etc.), p. 19. (Ch. VI, p. 98.)

86 At least so long as No. 1040 of St. Ludkevec: *Etnografichny Zbirnek*, Vol. XXI, 1906, remains an isolated example. (Ch. VI, p. 98.)

87 J. Horváth: *A középkori magyar vers ritmusa* [The Rhythm of Hungarian Medieval Verse]. 1928, pp. 50 and 114. More recently, L. Vargyas dealt with folk and literary variants: *A magyar vers ritmusa* [The Rhythm of Hungarian Verse]. 1952, Ch. III: 'A kanásztánc' [The Swineherd's Dance]; 'Egy népi táncdaltípus ritmusának tanulságai' [The Lessons to Be Drawn from the Rhythm of a Folk-Dance Melody]. *Új Zenei Szemle*, 1951/4–5, pp. 34–51; *Magyar vers — magyar nyelv* [Hungarian Verse—Hungarian Language]. 1966, pp. 28–36. According to him, alternation in the number of syllables in this form is a Hungarian peculiarity, particularly in the four-line old-style melodies. The descendants of the medieval goliard songs must be sought in the rigid 4/4/4/2 and 4/4/4/3 rhythm, particularly two-line melodies of alien character. (Ch. VI, p. 99.)

88 This tune is also to be found in Rumanian *Colinda* songs. See Bartók: *Melodien der rumänischen Colinde*. Vienna, 1935, No. 49. Moravian variants are to be found in Sušil (p. 436) and Bartoš–Janáček (1901, p. XIX and No. 459). See also B. Rajeczky: 'Népdaltörténet és gregorián kutatás' [The History of Folksong and Gregorian Research] in *Kodály Em-*

lékkönyv [Memorial volume for the 60th birthday of Z. Kodály]. 1943, pp. 308–312. (Ch. VII, p. 100.)

89 The *Song-Book* of István Gálszécsi (1536) cannot be regarded as a collection of popular hymns. (Ch. VII, p. 101.)

90 P. Aubry: *Trouvères et Troubadours*, p. 112. It is known that Savonarola wrote religious texts to carnival tunes 'so as to take the Devil's songs away from him.' See Knud Jeppesen: *Die mehrstimmige italienische Laude um 1500*. Leipzig, 1935, p. XVII. (Ch. VII, p. 101.)

91 *Nagyszalontai gyűjtés. Magyar népköltési gyűjtemény* [Nagyszalonta Collection. Collection of Hungarian Folk Poetry], Vol. XIV, 1924, p. 290. (Ch. VII, p. 102.)

92 'Árokszállásnál volt egy veszedelem' [There was danger at Árokszállás]. Quoted by Dénes Bartha with variants in *A XVIII. század magyar dallamai* [Hungarian Songs of the 18th Century]. 1935, No. 116. See also his edition of the song-collection of Ádám Pálóczi-Horváth, No. 265. (Ch. VII, p. 102.)

93 Kodály: *Magyar Népzene* [Hungarian Folk Music], No. 29. (Ch. VII, p. 102.)

94 Two variants of this tune are included in the *Vietorisz MS.* (c. 1680). See B. Szabolcsi: *Probleme der alten ungarischen Musikgeschichte*, p. 24, No. 17 and p. 30, No. 35; also his *A XVII. század magyar világi dallamai* [Hungarian Secular Songs of the 17th Century], 1950, No. 54. (Ch. VII, p. 103.)

95 Given by B. Sztankó in 'A lőcsei tabulaturáskönyv choreái' [The Dances of the Lőcse Manuscript]. *Zenei Szemle*, Vol. XI (1926–7), p. 166 ff. and B. Szabolcsi's *Hungarian Secular Songs of the 17th Century*, No. 19. A Moravian variant is in Sušil (p. 452). (Ch. VII, p. 103.)

96 In Márk Kovács's *Song Book* of 1842, Vol. III, p. 86 and in Zsasskovszky: *Egyházi énektár* [Collection of Church Songs]. 1855, 289. (Ch. VII, p. 104.)

97 In Harmat–Sík's 'Szent vagy, Uram!' (Roman Catholic Hymnbook), No. 38; Bartók; *Hungarian Folk Music*, No. 192. This tune has also been borrowed by the Rumanian *Colindas*, see: Bartók: *Rumanian Colinda Tunes*, No. 100. (Ch. VII, p. 104.)

98 Zsasskovszky: *Egyházi énektár* (Hymnbook). 1855, p. 258. An expanded form is to be found in 'Szent vagy, Uram!' No. 294. Quoted by Dénes Bartha, from eighteenth-century MSS., in *Hungarian Songs of the Eighteenth Century*, No. 160. (Ch. VII, p. 104.)

99 Printed for the first time in Füredi's *100 Magyar népdal* [100 Hungarian Folksongs]. 1851, No. 74; it had already been sung on 3rd March, 1848, in the play *Párbaj, mint isten-ítélet* [A Duel as Divine Judgement]. The music was written by Béni Egressy, and it seems that he transformed the psalm melody, perhaps unconsciously. Much of his time was devoted to composing organ-settings of the psalms; the Manuscript Room of the Hungarian National Museum has 51 such works by him. (A setting of the 134th Psalm is not among them.) (Ch. VII, p. 105.)

100 It is not certain that this is the work of Jacopone, but all Hungarian books give him as the author. See Dreves-Blume: *Ein Jahrtausend lateinischer Hymnendichtung*, Vol. II, p. 425. (Ch. VII, p. 105.)

101 1582, p. CLIX. (Ch. VII, p. 105.)

102 *Cantus Catholici*, 1651, pp. 143 and 249. (Ch. VII, p. 105.)

103 With complete text. *Transylvanian Folksongs*, No. 66. (Ch. VII, p. 105.)

104 *Das katholische deutsche Kirchenlied*, Vol. II, p. 316. (Ch. VII, p. 105.)

105 Kolozsvár, 1751, p. 460. This is the only Latin hymn in the Kolozsvár hymnbook. The Hungarian translation is given on p. 461. (Ch. VII, p. 105.)

106 *Halottas énekek* [Funeral Songs]. Debrecen, 1791, p. 178. Funeral songs are generally those best known among the peasantry. A glance through a hymnbook reveals that the most thumb-marked pages are those containing funeral hymns. (Ch. VII, p. 105.)

107 *Pisny Evangelistskych*, etc., 1576, p. 425. Zahn: *Die Melodien der deutschen ev. Kirchenlieder*, No. 1171 (1566). The other tune is on p. 797 (Zahn, No. 4966). (Ch. VII, p. 106.)

108 Together with other Bukovina Hungarians, the inhabitants of this village settled in 1941 in Bács-Bodrog, and later in Tolna County. (Ch. VII, p. 107.)

109 In the 1564 edition of the *Pisny Evangelistskych*, the 20th note is not b but f_2, that is, a second instead of a downward leap of a sixth. It is possible that b is the original, and that the descending sixth is a printer's error. Zahn (No. 4966, in the 1566 hymnbook of the Bohemian Brethren) also gives a form without the sixth. (Ch. VII, p. 107.)

110 Th. Gérold: *La musique au moyen âge*. 1932, p. 231. Cf. Zahn, No. 1160; on p. 722 of the 1576 hymnbook mentioned in note 98. Moravian variant in Sušil, p. 513, No. 705. Slovak variant, *Slow. Spevy*, Vol. II, p. 366. (Ch. VII, p. 107.)

111 Budapest University Library, MS. A 112. (Ch. VII, p. 108.)

112 See 'Szent vagy, Uram!', No. 180. (Ch. VII, p. 108.)

113 Published in facsimile by M. Schneider, 1924. (Ch. VII, p. 109.)

114 Ed. Ladislaus Juhász, Lipsiae, 1934. B. G. Teubner IV. XX Bibliotheca scriptorum medii recentisque aevorum, Saec. XV. Caput 17, p. 18: 'Hungari enim sive nobiles sive rustici sint, eadem fere verborum condicione utuntur et sine varietate loquuntur, eadem enim pronuntiatio, eadem vocabula, similes accentus ubique sunt... Sed apud Hungaros, ut diximus, eadem loquendi forma vel exigua admodum differentia est, unde fit, ut carmen lingua Hungarica compositum rusticis et civibus mediis et extremis eodem tenore intelligatur.' (Ch. VII, p. 109.)

115 Published by Z. Ferenczi in the *Régi magyar könyvtár* [Old Hungarian Series]. 1899, p. 34. It would of course be absurd to maintain that this new edition was responsible for its spread. The source of this tune was Kolon (Nyitra County), 1906. (Ch. VII, p. 110.)

116 See Gábor Mátray: *Történeti, bibliai és gúnyoros magyar énekek dallamai a XVI. századból* [Hungarian Historical, Biblical, and Satirical Songs of the 16th Century]. 1859, p. 6. Also Bence Szabolcsi: *A XVI. század magyar históriás zenéje* [Hungarian Epic Song of the 16th Century]. 1931, Appendix I. (Ch. VII, p. 110.)

117 K. Thaly: *Vitézi énekek* [Songs of Heroes]. 1864, Vol. II, p. 283. János Buda published a carefully revised and accurate edition of the *Szencsei MS*. Budapest, 1943. (Ch. VII, p. 111.)

118 Ph. E. M. No. 433a. (Ch. VII, p. 111.)

119 Given in Dénes Bartha: *Hungarian Songs of the Eighteenth Century*, No. 50 and in his edition of the Song-Book of Ádám Pálóczi-Horváth, 1953, No. 191. (Ch. VII, p. 111.)

120 See Kodály: *Néprajz és zenetörténet* [Ethnography and Musical History]. 1933. (Ch. VII, p. 111.)

121 See Kodály: *Árgirus nótája* [Argirus' Song]. 1921. (Ch. VII, p. 112.)

122 More or less closely related examples are:

Somogyi táncok (Dances of Somogy) 1954, p. 259, No. 53/k. Csurgó (Somogy County),
Swineherd's dance performed on violin. L. V.

204

Bolhás (Somogy County). K.

205

Hej két ti - kom   ta - va - li,   há - rom har-mad - é - vi,

Ha   tud - tá - tok,   hogy az   e - nyém,   mért ad - ta - tok   en - ni?

Tyu-tyu sző - ke,   tyu-tyu bar - na,   tyu-tyu mind a   há - rom!

A   ka - ka - som   sem ve - szett el,   nincsen sem - mi   ká - rom.

Bartók, No. 303b. Felsőireg (Tolna County), 1907. B.

Tempo giusto ♩ = 84

206

N   Csóri kanász   mit főz-tél?   Tüdőt kaposz - tá - val.

Mi - vel   rántot - tál   be - le?   Ha - sa - sza - lon - ná - val.

Hát az   ö - reg   e - szik - e?   Tőtsd   ne - ki   tál - ba!

Ha   nem e - szik   be - lő - le,   vágd a   po - fá - já - hoł

(Ch. VII, p. 113.)

123 The text is given in one only of the old Hungarian song-books. See K. Szabó: *Bibliography of Old Hungarian Literature*, Vol. I, p. 342 and P. Erdélyi: *Énekeskönyveink* [Hungarian Song-Books]. 1899, No. 66. (Ch. VII, p. 113.)

124 See B. Szabolcsi: *Probleme der alten ungarischen Musikgeschichte*. 1926, p. 21 and *Die ungarischen weltlichen Melodien des 17. Jahrhunderts*. 1950, No. 13. In the so-called *Komáromi énekeskönyv* [Komárom Song-Book] Manuscript, Széchényi Library, Oct. Hung. 483, this song has a mixture of 3- and 4-line strophes. As the manuscript has obviously been used and appears not to have been copied from another, it was presumably sung in this way. (Ch. VII, p. 113.)

125 The text of the Moldavian song had already been changed, but the tune resembles the seventeenth-century form. Dénes Bartha: *Die ungarischen Melodien des 18. Jahrhunderts*, No. 29, quotes a variant noted at the end of the eighteenth century. Szabolcsi: *Probleme...*, p. 28, No. 29, indicates extant modern variants of another tune from the *Vietorisz MS.* The characteristic repetition of the $^3/_4$ bar occurs also in Bartók: *Hungarian Folk Music*, No. 258. (Ch. VII, p. 113.)

126 *Irodalomtörténeti Közlemények* [Publications of Literary History], 1909, p. 395. (Ch. VII, p. 114.)

127 *Transylvanian Folksongs*, Nos. 10, 23, 28, 124, 125. (Ch. VII, p. 116.)

128 *Ibid*. No. 37. (Ch. VII, p. 116.)

129 See T. Harsányi: 'Két koldusének forrása' [The Sources of Two Beggar's Songs]. *Ethnographia*, 1915, pp. 138 and 307. (Ch. VII, p. 116.)

130 *Transylvanian Folksongs*, No. 76; Bartók: *Hungarian Folk Music*, No. 188. (Ch. VII, p. 117.)

131 Thaly (*op. cit.*, in note No. 117), Vol. II, p. 91. One of the tunes linked with this text is No. 27 of Kodály's *A magyar népzene* [Hungarian Folk Music] (songs with piano accompaniment). (Ch. VII, p. 117.)

132 Cf., for example, *Transylvanian Folksongs*, No. 36 with a tune preserved by chance in a chapbook of 1749: *Zenei lexikon* [Musical Lexicon], Vol. II, pp. 67–68. The tune of 'Tegnap gróf halála' [Yesterday I was saddened by the Count's death], preserved in the *Kájoni MS.* and *Vietorisz MS.* from the seventeenth century, appears in a new and familiar light when it is compared with a recently found Transylvanian folksong. See *Irodalomtörténeti Közlemények*, 1909, p. 290, and Szabolcsi: *Probleme...*, p. 23, No. 14, *Secular Songs of the Seventeenth Century*, No. 15, and *Transylvanian Folksongs*, No. 110. (Ch. VII, p. 118.)

133 See Thoinot Arbeau: *Orchesographia*. 1588. (Ch. VII, p. 118.)

134 Á. Kiss: *Collection of Hungarian Children's Games*, p. 271, in 2/4 time; cf. Bartók: *Hungarian Folk Music*, Nos. 15, 316, and 209. Further variants: CMPH Vol. I, No. 1095, etc. For the more extended form, see CMPH Vol. III, No. 439 ff. (Ch. VII, p. 118.)

135 Published in *Régi magyar könyvtár* [Old Hungarian Library], Vol. II, p. 79. (Ch. VII, p. 118.

136 *A kótából való klavírozás mestersége, melyet készített az abban gyönyörködők kedvéért Gáti István, Budán, A' királyi Univerzitásnak betűivel* [The art of playing the pianoforte from music, prepared for the pleasure of amateurs, by István Gáti, Buda, printed by the Royal University]. 1802, p. 99. There is a variant in Ádám Pálóczi-Horváth's collection, 1813, No. 406,

which is almost identical, note for note. For J. Kócsi Patkó (1763–1842), see *Zenei Lexikon* [Musical Lexikon], Vol. II, p. 325. (Ch. VII, p. 119.)

137 János Sylvester: *Új Testamentum magyar nyelven* [New Testament in the Hungarian Language]. Published by Béla Varjas, 1960. (Facsimile) Part II, on (unnumbered) p. 164a. (Ch. VII, p. 121.)

138 F. S. Kraus: *Anthropophyteia*, Vol. II, Leipzig, 1905, pp. 125–153, and Vol. III, 1906. pp. 51–60. (Ch. VII, p. 121.)

139 János Horváth: 'Hír három virágénekről' [News of Three 'Flower Songs']. *Magyar Nyelv* [Hungarian Language], 1949, Ch. I, p. 10. (Ch. VII, p. 122.)

140 *Magyar Nyelv* [Hungarian Language], 1929, p. 88. (Ch. VII, p. 122.)

141 CMPH Vol. II, No. 254. Cf. Eckhardt: *Az utolsó virágének* [The Last 'Flower Song']. Minerva Series, No. 27, 1930. (Ch. VII, p. 122.)

142 J. Kriza: *Vadrózsák* [Wild Roses], No. 248. Tune, *Transylvanian Folksongs*, No. 3. The text was recorded as early ad the mid-sixteenth century, see *Új Zenei Szemle*, 1952, No. 3, p. 11. (Ch. VII, p. 123.)

143 But Pázmány's strictures would seem to apply rather more to art poetry, since he discusses the authors as well. (Sermons, II, p. 261.) 'And what better name than universal procurers for those who contaminate the people by composing "flower songs"? Not content with their own depravity, they lay traps for others, and so inflame all the evil passions that are roused by reading or hearing such songs; no punishment is too severe for them.' Elsewhere he says (Sermons, III, p. 263): 'Blessed God! What would these godly people say about our own times! When men of every kind make show of their wit and skill by scribbling vile "flower songs" that young women and children know from memory; there is scarcely a house that does not resound with them.' Here the spirit of the Counter-Reformation is in contrast with that of Sylvester who, living a century earlier, still felt the breath of the Renaissance. The various Churches have maintained an unchanged attitude on this question almost up to our own day. See, for example, the moral tract *A'keresztények között ez idő szerént uralkodó romlottságnak kútfejeiről* [Concerning the Origins of the Present Universal Corruption in Christendom]. Debrecen, 1735, Vol. II, p. 289: 'What is the significance of these numberless books on love, these many love songs? All spring from the widespread lewdness and debauchery now holding sway.' — Tolstoy's attitude to love poetry is not very different from this. (See his essay *What Is Art?*, etc.) (Ch. VII, p. 124.)

144 Bálint Sárosi: *Die Volksmusikinstrumente Ungarns*. Leipzig, 1967 in *Handbuch der europäischen Volksmusikinstrumente*. Edited by Ernst Emsheimer and Erich Stockmann, Series I, Vol. 1. (Ch. VIII, p. 125.)

145 See the article by K. Viski in *A magyarság néprajza*, Vol. II, p. 375 ff. (Ch. VIII, p. 126.)

146 In Bukovina gipsy villages, even the most famous gipsy-band leader ploughs his land single-handed. (Ch. VIII, p. 127.)

147 *Ethnographia*, 1910, p. 297 ff. J. Bihari's *15 ungarische Tänze für 2 Violinen*, published by Artaria in Vienna *c.* 1808, have seemingly preserved traces of both these primitive forms of accompaniment. (Ch. VIII, p. 127.)

148 See Sándor Ujfalvy: *Az erdélyi régebbi és közelebbi vadászatok* [Ancient and Modern Hunting

in Transylvania]. Cluj, 1927, p. 33. On p. 8, there is a mention of an orchestra of 2 violins, cello, *tárogató* (originally a shawm, but since 1890 a soprano saxophone-like instrument) and cymbalum. Gvadányi also notes gipsy bands composed of 5 or 6 players in *A' mostan folyó ország gyűlésének satyrice critice való leírása* [A Critical-Satirical Description of the Present National Assembly]. 1791, pp. 179 and 255. The title-page of *Six Hungarian Melodies* by A. Berners (1808) shows 2 violinists, a viola player, a cellist, and a cymbalum-player. Baron von Prónay's 'Ungarischer Tanz' (published in the 1840s in the periodical *Honderű*) has a drawing by Barabás showing a 4-man ensemble: violin, clarinet, cymbalum, and cello. This drawing is plagiarized on the title-page of a *csárdás* by Ignác Frank, 'Apám nótája' [My Father's Tune], 1863. The same ensemble appears in the well-known painting by Ágost Canzi: *Vintage in the Neighbourhood of Vác* (1859), in the Museum of Fine Arts, Budapest, and also of Mérty's *Szegzárdi szüreti csárdás* [Csárdás at the Wine-harvest of Szekszárd] (1861). The same four players appear again in the title-page drawing of two *csárdás* pieces by Mérty, 'Kalocsai emlék' [Memories of Kalocsa] and 'Cserebogár' [Cockchafer]. A gipsy band composed of five players is shown in a drawing by Grimm, in Kubinyi-Vahot's *Magyarország és Erdély képekben* [Hungary and Transylvania in Pictures]. 1853, p. 100; a band of three (violin, shawm [*tárogató*], and cymbalum) appears on the title-page of Füredi's *Hundred Hungarian Folksongs*, 1851. Count István Fáy's *Régi magyar zene gyöngyei* [Gems of Old Hungarian Music] shows in Rózsavölgyi's edition an ensemble of three violins, cymbalum, shawm *(tárogató)*, cello and double-bass. Even in 1896, the title-page of Miska Lengyel's *Gipsy March* shows only 7 or 8 players. The gipsy band in the *Echt ungarische Nationaltänze* of 'Jántsy von Lotz' [Jancsi Lóci] has nine players. (Third issue, Haslinger Press, No. 5531; there is a copy in the library of the Hungarian National Museum.) The instruments are: 5 violins, 2 clarinets, 1 double-bass. The ninth player is standing in the background and his instrument cannot be seen. Systematic collation of these pictures would be a valuable piece of research. (Ch. VII, p. 127.)

149 B. Bartók: 'A magyar nép hangszerei' [Hungarian Folk Instruments]. *Ethnographia*, 1911, p. 305. Recollections of these examples appear in the armoury scene of *Bluebeard's Castle*. (Ch. VIII, p. 128.)

150 *Ethnographia*, 1907, p. 154. (Ch. VIII, p. 130.)

151 There is a single specimen of the 4-hole shepherd's pipe *(furulya)* in the Budapest Ethnographical Museum. Its basic scale is *e-f-g-a-b*. (Ch. VIII, p. 130.)

152 'A palóc duda' [The Palóc Bagpipe]. *Néprajzi Múzeum Értesítője*, 1934, pp. 81–88, printed separately in 1935. Partly at the suggestion of the town clerk, the Chief Magistrate of Nógrád County, B. Soldos, drew up a list of bagpipers in his jurisdiction: 23 were reported, but the real figure may well have been higher. (This information was kindly su pplied by László Madarassy.) This was in spite of the fact that such an authority as the folklorist Gyula Pap was complaining in 1865 that the bagpipe was dying out (*Palóc népköltemények* [Palóc Folk Poems], p. XVIII). For shepherd bagpipers, see the poems of J. Kőműves, 1861, p. 104. Lajos Vargyas: *Régi népdalok Kiskunhalasról* [Old Folksongs from Kiskunhalas]. Budapest, 1954, pp. 10–12 described the life of a bagpiper from a town on the Great Plain, who played at weddings and other occasions in the farming region between the

Tisza and the Danube. About 1939, he participated in folk-ensemble performances. (Ch. VIII, p. 133.)

153 So described by István Geleji Katona in the introduction to *Öreg graduál* [Old Gradual], 1636: 'Az orgonán értvén minden fúvós és tömlős sípokat az minemű a' Magyaroknak első Musicaljok, az bordo síp avagy duda is.' [By 'organ' I mean all pipes with bellows and bags, including the chief musical instrument of the Magyars, the bourdon pipe or bagpipe.] (Ch. VIII, p. 133.)

154 In his book *Jánoshidai avarkori kettőssíp* [The Double Pipe at the Time of the Jánoshida Avars], Budapest, 1934, Dénes Bartha made a comprehensive collection of international comparative material about musical instruments of the bagpipe class. (Ch. VIII, p. 134.)

155 Compare *Larousse de la musique*, Paris, 1957, heading *Vielle à roue:* '... répandu sporadiquement en Europe, des pays nordiques à l'Italie et de l'Angleterre aux pays slaves.' (Ch. VIII, p. 134.)

156 *Zeneközlöny*, 1911, p. 309. *Zenei Lexikon* [Musical Lexicon], Vol. II, p. 60. See also Zoltán Trócsányi: 'A nyenyere Magyarországon' [The Hurdy-Gurdy in Hungary]. *Új barázda*, 1933; Béla Avasi: 'Quelques données sur la vielle hongroise.' *Acta Ethnographica*, 1959, pp. 293–307. (Ch. VIII, p. 135.)

157 Lajos Vargyas: 'Magyar népdalok francia párhuzamai' [French Parallels of Hungarian Folksongs]. *Néprajzi Közlemények*, V/3–4 (1960) pp. 3–18. (Ch. VIII, p. 136.)|

158 In the work quoted in Note No. 136, István Gáti was already aware of this phenomenon; p. 49: 'Hungarian tunes often resemble Slovak, Cossack, Turkish and Rumanian tunes. Many Cossack and Slovak dances can be danced to Hungarian tunes and Hungarian dances to several Slovak tunes, but Hungarian dances cannot be danced so well to German tunes, nor German dances to Hungarian tunes.' (Ch. VIII, p. 137.)

159 *Zenei Lexikon* [Musical Lexikon], Vol. III, p. 68. (Ch. VIII, p.137 .)

160 B. Szabolcsi: *Probleme...*, p. 21 and *Hungarian Secular Songs of the Seventeenth Century*, No. 4. (Ch. VIII, p. 137.)

161 See Note No. 118. (Ch. VIII, p. 137.)

162 Another form of the Csíksomlyó variant appears in Bartalus's collection *(Hungarian Folksongs*, Vol. IV, No. 121). It is included with religious texts in L. Amade's *Istenes énekek* [Godly Songs], 1755 (Négyessy edition, p. 519). The German variant: Zahn: *Die Melodie der deutschen evangelischen Kirchenlieder*, Vol. IV, 7341a, dates from 1739. This was adopted as the tune of a funeral chant of the Hungarian Reformed Church: 'Búcsút vennem' [I must take leave of this world] ; it appears for the first time in A. Kovács's MS. (Széchényi Library, Oct. Hung. 534, 1767–1777, p. 28a), and Losontzi's *Halotti énekek* [Songs for the Dead]. (Pest, 1778, p. 34). All these differ from the variant of the *Vietorisz MS.* in that their last 4 or 5 notes are a third higher, producing a decidedly major character. It is possible that theirs is the original version, and that the tune in the *Vietorisz MS.* is a Hungarian development. But it cannot be definitely decided, since there is no foreign evidence prior to 1739. Roman Catholic hymnbooks have a minor variant (M. Kovács, 1842, Vol. II, p. 16; 'Szent vagy, Uram!' No. 234). See also: Dénes Bartha: *Hungarian Songs of the Eighteenth Century* (No. 32)—a manuscript variant from the end of the eighteenth century. (Ch. VIII, p. 137.)

163 Vol. 56, p. 52. (Ch. VIII, p. 139.)

164 *Ethnographia*, 1910, p. 297. (Ch. VIII, p. 139.)

165 These four bars exist in almost every *csůrdöngölő*. For the third tune, see *Ethnographia*, 1910, p. 297, for the second, see Bartalus: *Hungarian Folksongs*, Vol. I, No. 99. The fourth was taken down by the author in 1910 from a gipsy in Gyergyóalfalu. Data from earlier writings about still extant folk-music pieces are at present lacking; hence it is worth mentioning that two of the dances of the *Kájoni MS.* (one by Kelemen Mikes) and one other (see *Irodalomtörténeti Közlemények*, 1909, p. 393 and p. 388, No. 13; also Szabolcsi: *Hungarian Secular Songs of the Seventeenth Century*, Nos. 29 and 23) appeared in Bartók's Maramureş collection, *Die Volksmusik der Rumänen von Maramureş.* Munich, 1923, p. 170, No. 185, and p. 167, No. 182a and b. (Ch. VIII, p. 139.)

166 Radloff: *Proben der Volksliteratur der türkischen Stämme* (X. Mundarten der bessarabischen Gagausen). St. Petersburg, 1904, Music Appendix. (Ch. VIII, p. 140.)

167 Cf. Lajos Vargyas: 'Die Wirkung des Dudelsacks auf die ungarische Volkstanzmusik.' *Studia Memoriae Belae Bartók Sacra 1956*, pp. 503–540. With more examples (in Hungarian): *A MTA Nyelv- és Irodalomtudományi Osztályának Közleményei*, VIII/1–4, 1956, pp. 241–291. (Ch. VIII, p. 140.)

168 Lajos Vargyas: *Áj falu zenei élete* [The Musical Life of the Village of Áj]. Budapest, 1941. A brief summary of results is given in: 'Das Musikleben im ungarischen Dorf und die Methoden seiner Erforschung.' *Deutsches Jahrbuch für Volkskunde*, 1957, pp. 447–469. The complete folksong material has also been published: *Áj falu zenei anyaga* [The Musical Material of the Village of Áj], Vol. I. *Régi népdalok* [Old Folksongs], *Néprajzi Közlemények* V/2 (1960); II. *Új népdalok* [New Folksongs], the same source VI/3–4 (1961) and VIII/1 (1963). The art-song material remains to be published. Pál Járdányi: *A kidei magyarság világi zenéje* [The Secular Music of the Hungarians in the Village of Kide]. Kolozsvár, 1943. István Halmos: *A zene Kérsemjénben* [Music in Kérsemjén]. Budapest, 1959. (App. I, p. 148.)

PLACE NAMES

The vast majority of the folksongs contained in this book were collected by Zoltán Kodály, Béla Bartók and other collectors before the First World War.

As all previous publications have used Hungarian forms of place names which have since been changed, it would complicate matters to alter them. Hence they appear in this book in the form originally used by the collectors. The same applies to the names of counties.

The following is a list of place names that have changed since the collections were made. The Hungarian county is put in brackets after the place name.

Andrásfalva (formerly Bukovina)	Măneuţi (Rumania)
Ábrahám (Udvarhely)	Avrameşti (Rumania)
Barslédec (Bars)	Ladice (Czechoslovakia)
Berencs (Nyitra)	Berenč (Czechoslovakia)
Bodóka (Trencsén)	Krivosud Bodovka (Czechoslovakia)
Csíkjenőfalva (Csík)	Ineu Ciuc (Rumania)
Csíksomlyó (Csík)	Sumulen (Rumania)
Csíkszenttamás (Csík)	Tomeşti Ciuc (Rumania)
Dolha (Máramaros)	Dolhoje (U.S.S.R.)
Farkasd (Nyitra)	Farkasd (Czechoslovakia)
Ghymes (Nyitra)	Dymeš (Czechoslovakia)
Gicce (Gömör)	Hucín (Czechoslovakia)
Gyergyócsomafalva (Csík)	Ciumani (Rumania)
Gyergyóremete (Csík)	Remetea (Rumania)
Gyergyószentmiklós (Csík)	Gheorgheni (Rumania)
Gyergyóújfalu (Csík)	Joseni (Rumania)
Gyímesközéplok (Csík)	Lunea de jos (Rumania)
Hadikfalva (formerly Bukovina)	Dorneşti (Rumania)
Ipolyság (Hont)	Šahy (Czechoslovakia)
Istensegíts (formerly Bukovina)	Tibeni (Rumania)

Józseffalva (formerly Bukovina)	Vorniceni (Rumania)
Karcfalva (Csík)	Cîrța (Rumania)
Kászonfeltíz (Csík)	Plăești de sus (Rumania)
Kászonújfalu (Csík)	Cașin (Rumania)
Kénos (Udvarhely)	Sulfureni (Rumania)
Kolon (Nyitra)	Kolíňany (Czechoslovakia)
Komárom (Komárom)	Komárno (Czechoslovakia)
Lécped (Moldva)	Lespezi (Rumania)
Lukanénye (Hont)	Luka Nanince (Czechoslovakia)
Magyargyerőmonostor (Kolozs)	Mănăstarul Unguresc (Rumania)
Menyhe (Nyitra)	Mehynce (Czechoslovakia)
Nagygut (Bereg)	Nagygut (Czechoslovakia)
Nagymegyer (Komárom)	Vel'ký Meder (Czechoslovakia)
Nagypeszek (Hont)	Vel'ký Pesek (Czechoslovakia)
Nagyszalonta (Bihar)	Salonta Mare (Rumania)
Nyárádköszvényes (Maros-Torda)	Matrici (Rumania)
Perjése (Gömör)	Dražice (Czechoslovakia)
Rafajnaújfalu (Bereg)	Rafajnovo (U.S.S.R.)
Sepsiszentgyörgy (Háromszék)	Sfîntul Gheorghe (Rumania)
Somoska (formerly Bakó, Moldavia)	Valea Mare (Bacău, Rumania)
Szárhegy (Csík)	Lăzărea (Rumania)
Székelyudvarhely (Udvarhely)	Odorhei (Rumania)
Szilágyperecsen (Szilágy)	Perecein (Rumania)
Tekerőpatak (Csík)	Valea Strîmbă (Rumania)
Udvarhelyszék (Udvarhely)	Odorhei (Rumania)
Vacsárcsi (Csík)	Văcăeşci (Rumania)
Zalaba (Hont)	Zalaba (Czechoslovakia)
Zobor (Zobor region, Nyitra County)	Zubor (Czechoslovakia)
Zsére (Nyitra)	Žirány (Czechoslovakia)
Csallóköz	Žitny Ostrov (Czechoslovakia)
Erdély (Transylvania)	Transylvania (Rumania)
Muraköz (Zala) area between the rivers Mur and Drava	Medjumurie (Yugoslavia)

TRANSLATION OF THE SONG TEXTS

The aim in translating the song texts has been to give a clear rendering of the sense rather than to indulge in poetic effects of rhythm or vocabulary. Line for line, the English text follows the Hungarian, and any necessary amplification or explanation has been put in brackets. For the sake of uniformity, names of people, places and rivers have been left as in Hungarian, except that names are given in the English order, with the surname last. In all folksongs there are untranslatable colloquialisms, plays on words, and passages made complex by obscure symbolism, or as a result of the age-long process of oral transmission. In such cases, wherever possible, a suitable English idiomatic equivalent has been used. Within the limits of stylistic unity, the translators have tried to keep the individual flavour of such passages, and so to convey some idea of the linguistic variety of the original.

Hungarian pronunciation may be briefly summarized as follows: The stress is always on the first syllable. Short '*a*' is pronounced as in *what; sz=s, c=ts, s=sh, zs=s* as in *pleasure, cs=ch, y* softens the preceding consonant and is pronounced together with it, for example, *egy [one]=edge.*

II There's but one lovely girl in the world,
  She's my beloved sweetheart,
  God must love me very much,
  That he has given you to me.

1 The cart rattles,
  Jancsi cracks his whip,
  Perhaps they're coming for me!
  Alas, sweet mother,
  Beloved one, who nursed me,
  Soon they'll carry me away!

3 Over the vineyard on the hill
  Walks the girl with her little brother,
  From the Danube the wind blows.
  Whenever the wind blows from the Danube,
  It always catches the poor man—
  From the Danube the wind blows.

4 Oh, from the Danube blows the wind, Lie beside me
      and it won't reach you,
  From the Danube blows the wind.
  If it didn't blow from the Danube, Then it wouldn't
      be cold,
  From the Danube blows the wind.

7 The peacock alighted on the County Hall,
  But brought no release for the prisoners.

8 Éva, darling Éva,
  Now the plums are growing ripe,
  They are strewn upon the ground,
  We'll have them picked by daybreak.

9 Red apples gleam on the hilltop,
  A lass with a yellow kerchief goes walking in the meadow.
  Lovely is the meadow, made lovely by the flowers,
  Or rather, by that lass with the yellow kerchief.

10 The pig peeps from the copse, only his ears can be seen.
The swineherd dallies with young women in the bush.
The sow has been lost and her nine piglets with her,
After her goes the swineherd with an empty knapsack.

11 The sound of a bagpipe comes
From the far end of the garden.
A shepherd lad is playing
With grief-stricken heart.

12 I'm off, I'm off,
I'll never look back —
I, in this village,
Will never live again.

13 I have got married, Miska,
I have a wife—Aniska.
She's clean enough, as clean as can be—
She sweeps up twice a month.

14 You can tell a swineherd
By his odd gait,
By the criss-cross thongs of his moccasins,
By the strap of his knapsack.

Hey, pig, get out of the copse,
Only his ears can be seen.
The young swineherd, under the bush,
Is dallying with a young woman.

15 Thank goodness, there are acorns here,
The little boar will now grow fat.
When he's fattened we will kill him
And into the knapsack he'll go.

16 O rosemary, rosemary,
My shirt's torn off my back.
I've now got someone at Kövesd, though,
Who will mend my shirt for me.

17a I have no father nor mother,
　　　God is angry with me.
　　　I am orphaned, like a lonely stork
　　　That has no one to take his part.

　b The soldier's walking down the street,
　　　Anna Mónár stands in the farmyard.
　　　'Hey!' says the soldier,
　　　'Come with me, Anna Mónár.'

18 I had a goat—did you know?
　　　Fenced her in the garden—did you know?
　　　A wolf has eaten her—did you know?
　　　Left nothing but the horns—do you see?

19 The gipsy eats cheese-curd, duba,*
　　　Kicks up a row afterwards, lëba,*
　　　Then says he'll slap me in the face, duba,*
　　　Better to hit his grandpa, lëba.*

20 Over there a flower is opening,
　　　All night long I smell its scent:
　　　To whom shall I turn my dark eyes?
　　　Who will comfort my heart?

21 Heaven grant that somebody, somebody,
　　　To broach a cask, would send for me, would send for me!
　　　I would broach his cask, his cask,
　　　And drink up his good wine, good wine!

22 Load the waggon well, boy,
　　　Brushwood thorns will prick your palms,
　　　The more they prick the palms of your hands,
　　　The better you'll load up the waggon.

23 Where were you last night, titmouse?
　　　At your window, violet sweet.
　　　Why didn't you knock, titmouse?
　　　I feared your husband, violet sweet.

* Gipsy-sounding words.

24 My hat is floating down the Tisza,
   The village mayor holds my sheepskin-coat in pledge.
   But my heart is beating here,
   Its hot flames flicker towards you.

26 The bridge over the wide water is narrow, I shall fall in,
   I'll put you, dearest love, out of my head.
   Banish all thought of you from my mind.
   May Jesus repay you for your kindness.

27 I thought I should not have to be a soldier,
   And could take care of my mother dear.
   But now I see I must be a soldier,
   And wear the shako of Franz Josef.

28 I've never stolen in my life
   But six young bullocks in Debrecen;
   I drove the bullocks to my home,
   All six were iron-grey.

29 This side of the Tisza, beyond the Danube,
   Beyond the Tisza lives a horseherd with his herd.
   His small bay horse is tethered
   With a rope, without a rug, next to his master.

30 Today is the second day of Easter,
   As you well know,
   On the first day Jesus rose from the grave
   To be glorified.

31 If you're going to join the colours,
   Tell me, my son, where shall I find you?
   Come out to Galicia—
   And there you'll find me in an inn.

32 Dömbör voivod, Dömbör voivod, cricket-eared Goat.
       Your father was also a voivod master, little
       Lipic Kelemen.
   Six eggs in the hay loft, how did they come to be there?
       Let us make a ragged broth, there is no vinegar in it.

33 I lost my handkerchief, my mother will beat me for it.
   A fair-hair lad found it, he wants a kiss for it.
But he will give it to me, I'll kiss him for it,
   But he will give it to me, I'll kiss him for it,
Ai ai ai ai ai ai ai ai ai ai (etc., to the end).

36 My God, who am I waiting for?
I'm going to Budapest,
There I shall stroll about with the girls
Every Saturday night.

37 A maiden is fair for a while, For eighteen years,
But a lad is too, Until he gets married.

38 Every one lives with good fortune, Only I live in misery;
I bow my head silently, I just weep bitterly.

39 I was my mother's daughter
As long as I had no lover,
But as soon as I found a lover,
My mother disowned me.

40 Come along where I am going,
Then you'll see where I live,
Near a dog-rose bush—
Come, my sweet, I'll embrace you.

41a The acorns have dropped from the tree,
   I've just come from the farm,
   My shirt and linen trousers are dirty,
   As for me, I'm in love.

  b Stop tugging at me like that, mother:
   Have you no other worry about me (but that)?
   I have filled my pitcher full,
   The big killers have slain me.

42 The cat went to the pig-sticking;
The dog went after her,
The wolf went after the dog,
The cock went after the wolf.

43 My only sorrow is that I must part from you;
   Sorrow to have spent so much time running after you.

44 The road before me is weeping,
   The path lies in grief.
   It even calls out to me:
   'God bless you!'

45 The bitterness of grief,
   Even a brother is a foe.
   How can a stranger fail to be,
   When even a brother means you no good?

46 The bell is ringing for vespers,
   Come, friend, to the woods,
   To the top of the new road,
   To the top of the new road.

47 I am an orphan, with no one to help me!
   I mourn even for the water.
   I am an orphan, like the bird
   That flies above, over that cloud.

48 Oh, for two weeks now, or even three,
   I've been waiting for my head shepherd.
   Here he comes, now I see him,
   Astride a white-bellied donkey.

49 At daybreak on Thursday
   An attacker stands in my doorway.
   They are bringing the branding iron, Oh!
   My poor heart is about to break, Oh!

50 In eighteen forty-six
   I must go to war,
   If it is written
   That in battle I must fall.

51a The street-corner is curved,
   I have often passed by there.
   If I pass by again,
   I shall find my dearest love.

b Thirteen and a half... *
  I asked you to marry me, and you refused;
  As you didn't marry me, you stayed at home
  And became a mother of girls.

52 The fish pond, the fish pond of Vacsárcs, I fell into
      it with my horse, with my horse.
   Oh my Lord! Who will pull me out, oh who will pull
      me out? Is there anyone left to pity me?

53 Oh, how much I harvested this summer, How little I
      slept in my bed!
   Make your bed, my darling, make your festooned bed,
      Let me rest myself under it.

54 In the famous shop at Miskolc
   Hunter Jóska went a-shopping,
   Hunter Jóska went a-shopping,
   Dressed in violet cambric.

55a In Bosnia, the music's fine,
    The boys line up in rows,
    Each has his sweetheart with him,
    Only mine's gone far from me.

 b When I go dancing again,
   I'll fasten brass spurs to my boots.
   My brass spurs will jingle:
   'I had a love—I must forget her.'

56 Street, street, street in Szilice,
   For the last time I'm walking along it.
   For the last time I stop in front of a cottage,
   At the trellised gate of my dear love.

57 Beyond the water there's an enclosure,
   In it a bird struts up and down,
   I'm trying to catch him, but he won't wait,
   Oh, my God, what a pity!

*Original text: 'three apples and a half,' meaning: the suitor is not welcome. (If he is welcome, there are three apples on the plate.)

58 Fine thread, hard seed,
  What a proud fellow you are!
  You're in debt to all the world
  And master of less than a farthing.

59 An orphan am I, an orphan—
  God, too, sees that.
  May God the Father punish those
  Who harm an orphan.

60 (Oh) If only someone would propose to me (Oh!),
  And give me a silken veil!
  I wouldn't even care if he beat me every day,
  So long as I could be a fresh young wife.

62 The fire burns when it flickers,
  I live when I go stealing,
  I don't steal, I barter,
  But I have a real good life,
  Whoopee, but a real good life.

63 Ah, you should weep for me, mother, while I am with you.
  So you can weep for me, when I'm parted from you.
  Ah, the good Lord knows where I shall die,
  The good Lord knows where I shall die.

64 Over there did I work, I was a farm hand,
  I laid my head to rest under a rose-briar.

66 Kenderes is fenced round,
  Planted with small vine-stocks.
  My mare is saddled,
  I can ride wherever I please.

67a When the shepherd drinks wine, His grey-haired donkey
      is sad.
  Don't grieve, grey-haired donkey! We shall soon go
      after the flock.

  b My mother said to me, Why do you need a sweetheart?
   But I paid her no heed, I secretly kept one.

68 High above a swan is flying;
   A highwayman has been arrested,
   His name is Jóska Horváth,
   His hands and feet are put in chains.

69 A rosemary-bush that grows on the snow-capped rainbow-mountain
   Does not like where it is, and wants to go away,
   It must be taken from there and put in a new place,
   It must be taken from there and put in a new place.

76 My dear mother, darling mother! How could you
      go away from us,
   dear mother, so soon! Mother, mother,
   why does my mother not take pity on me, dear
   mother?

77 Where are you going, where are you going, Twelve Masons?
   We are going away, going away, If we can get work!

78 When you start out away from Transylvania, Don't look
      back, my sweetheart:
   Do not let it lie heavy on your heart, That you are
      going to a foreign land.

80a The King of Prussia is rightly angry
    That the enemy is campaigning in his country.
    The Russians are plundering his fine castles, fortresses and people,
    The King of Prussia is rightly angry.

  b There goes a young girl, carrying water on her shoulder,
    Followed by a cavalier leading a saddled horse.
    Stop there, stop there, lassie, give me a little water,
    I'll water my mare and then I'll embrace you.

  b₂ But I shall go away, and then I shall return.

81 I am a well-known highwayman,
   Jancsi is my name;
   The whole county is out hunting me,
   But it's no use their looking for me, for I can't be found,
   Only the girls visit the place where I'm staying.

82 I've just made a path
By which to go to Kolozsvár.
At a tavern in Kolozsvár
I drank up nine farthings' worth.

84 Our house has been painted white. The cymbalum player
   comes here every Saturday night.
He keeps on playing into my ear with his cymbalum:
   Remember your old sweetheart, dear lass!

85 Out on the edge of the village forget-me-nots bloom. I shall pick them,
   I shall pick them all, however many may bloom.
I shall pick them, I shall pick them, so as to be brought to your mind,
   I shall not even think of my old sweetheart.

89 A shepherd boy's playing his pipe in the field,
A fair-haired girl walks behind his flock.
Turn my flock back for me, fair-haired lass,
I will repay you for your trouble.

90 The farm hand's dead,
The farm hand's done for.
There's no one now to call out to the ox:
'Hey! Whoa! Rendes!'

91 Behind the gardens of Bolhás, Kata,
How many paths there are, Kata,
Every lad does make one and the same,
Through it he goes to his love, Kata.

94 Between two trees the moonshine gleamed;
I am like the camomile flower:
Half red, half white, half of this and half of that—
I shall die of so much bitter weeping.

95 Oh, may God damn the man who did this!
But even more the man who planned it!
They're taking away, they're taking away my darling from me,
To eat the unsalted bread of Franz Josef.

96 When I mount my white-stockinged horse
   I shall ride to the blacksmith's door.
   Blacksmith, open your smoky workshop door,
   And shoe my white-stockinged horse!

97 Above our house there's but one single star.
   That star is the envy of many.
   They grudge me that star, heigh-ho,
   That came down in front of our house.

98 It's struck one after midnight.
   Come sweetheart, see me out into the road!
   I'll see you out, yes, right to the middle of the road,
   I'll embrace you and kiss you lustily.

99 Could I but be a stroke of lightning,
   I would strike the recruiting office at Ipolynyék,
   I would smash up the Ipolynyék office, oh,
   That causes such misery to young men.

100a Hey, master, will you pay me off,
   I'm not going to tend your cattle anymore,
   I've got a job in the next county,
   As a horseherd with the horseherds.

  b Hey, master, will you pay me off,
   I'm not going to tend your flocks anymore,
   I've got a job in the next county,
   With the horseherds on the Plain.

101 Snail, snail, out you come, etc.

102 Snail, snail, out you come, etc.

103 Snail, snail, stick out your horns!

104 Töri-töri sóska,
   Zsidólegény csontja.*

*These lines have a sound value=Break, wood-sorrel, break The Jewish boy's bone.

108 Oats, oats for his horse,
   Pearls, pearls for his wife,
   A pearl necklace for his daughter,
   A cane switch for his son.

109a Play on, play on into sadness
   That his heart should break!
   He should remember once more,
   What he lied to his sweetheart a thousand times.

109b Uncle Pista, Uncle János,
   Take my chest outside for me.
   Take it, please, to the back of the garden,
   So no one carry it away.

110 I caught a gnat, it was bigger than a horse,
   I melted its fat—there was more than a hogshead.
   Who believes this is a bigger donkey than a horse,
   Who believes this is a bigger donkey than a horse.

111 Haycock bottom, haycock bottom, haycock rift, a roly-
       -poly woman in it,
   A roly-poly little spouse.
   Slowly, lightly, only quietly, embrace the one whom you love
   I embrace this, I prefer this, godmother's daughter.
   This Katica, this Nanica, colourful, colourful rose.
   Upon my head I placed my pearly basket, for I am the
       adopted daughter of my lady.
       oh, tulip's lovely flower of the Danube,
   Don't call me Ilona Tubi,
       just call me the fairest girl in the world,
   Two little goats dance, and they dance daintily.
   God grant us quiet rain, Juliska,
       let Mariska wash away both of them.
   Juliska will care for me, too, over here, and yonder.
   The candle burns when it is lit,
       oh, how nicely the girls dance it!

112a On this spot springs up a small grass plot,
   b Grazing on it is a magic young stag.
   c That magic young stag
   d Has a thousand branched horns.

e A thousand church candles
f Shall flare up when lit, go out when they are quenched.
g Haj, regö, rejtë.*
a Even that has been granted by the great God.
f Seven oxen, ancient law,
g Haj, regö, rejtë.
a Rise up, rise up, goodman,
g Haj, regö, rejtë.
a God has come down to your house.
g Haj, regö, rejtë.
f (On to) the servants and the multitudes,
e The filled cups
e (And) the laid tables.
a Even that has been granted by the great God.
g Haj, regö, rejtë.
a A buckled purse at the waist,
g Haj, regö, rejtë.
c Hundred and ten farthings in it
g Haj, regö, rejtë.
c Half of it for the poor singers,
d Half for the master,
g Haj, regö, rejtë.
c We shuffle and scuffle,
c Our moccasins are of oak-tree bark,
h Of buckwheat chaff our smocks, of oats our trousers.

113 May God grant this husbandsman
Two little oxen, etc.
Haj, regö, rejtë, even that has been granted by the great God.

114 Powdery snow is coming down, de hó reme róma.

115 Do not run, do not run, do not run, O our King Saint Stephen,
We are no devils, but thy subjects!
Haj, regö, rejtë, the great God can grant even that.
God grant this husbandsman
Two acres of ploughland, a hundred stock of wheat, haj regö, rajta,
Even that can be granted by the great God.

*'Regö, rejtë,' 'regö, rejtem,' 'de hó reme róma,' etc., are magic formulae that have lost meaning and now have no more than a rhythmical value. Haj=pron: hey.

116 Some footprints were seen on the ground here,
Whose house is this? A simple soul's.
A simple man lives in there.
Hej regö rejtem, rejtem...

117 Praised be Our Lord Jesus Christ! May God give you a peaceful night,
    my sweet husband!
Peaceful for us, and blissful for you.
Alas! I should never have thought, my dear, that we should so soon be
    parted!
Alas! only yesterday, about this time, you comforted me saying,
Don't you be afraid, wife, I'm not going to die, I'm not going to leave
    you yet!
Alas! my dearest, why have you left me behind in this sad world?

118 (The beginning is incomprehensible)
They were all married in gaiety, wearing white dresses, white wreaths
    and red headdresses,
But I alone was married in a black dress, green headdress (and) a green
    wreath,
And even then my gaiety did not last an hour,
I have never known a cheerful time since I was born into this world!
Alas! my sweet husband, my beloved protector,
I was with you scarcely two years,
I was with you scarcely two years,
And here I am, widowed already, etc.

119 Daughter, daughter, my darling Ilonka,
You have ended everything, leaving me with a great grief, etc.

120 Alas, dear aunt,
May God bless every speck of your dust, wherever it may fall!
Alas! you were always so true, so loving to us,
That maybe you even shared the birth-pangs with our dear mother!
Alas! dear, good aunt, you are half of my heart, half of my heart
Who helped my dear mother bring us up, etc.

121 Why did you leave me here, to live as a poor orphan,
my dearest mother, my kind mother, never-to-be-forgotten?
Why did you leave me behind as an orphan? Now I have
neither father nor mother, dearest mother! What word shall

186

I send to my dear father, my kind, never-to-be-forgotten father?

122 Alas, (mother-in-law,) how dearly we have loved each
other! We lived thirty-eight years under the same
roof, yet we didn't have much trouble with each
other. You have reared six children for us. You have
always looked after them faithfully.

123 Woe is me, (my God)! Who'll earn our daily bread,
my dearest, my husband? Who'll gather mushrooms
for me, field mushrooms and blewits? Who will earn
bread for my orphan children? (My God,) I don't
know what to do or where to go, my dearest, my
husband!

124 Alas, (my dearest,) my kindest man, who fell at the
front in 1944, who was killed by that damned war!
Alas, (Andrew,) where is your grave? Alas, where is your
mournful grave? I'll never be able to see your cross.

125 Now we say our last farewell to you; now we have
to leave you; from now on, we can see no more of
you but your grave. Good-bye, my dear, pretty
daughter, may you sleep in peace and have a quiet last rest!

126 Daddy, dear daddy, why did you leave me an orphan like
this? (Being an orphan,) it's all cups of bitterness.

127a Good evening, brown-haired lass. What has come over you?
Did your supper not agree with you?

   b My flowers, my flowers, my beautiful flowers,
Bow down to the earth and mourn for me.

128 How does the peasant sow
Gently the oats?
This is how the peasant sows
Gently the oats.

129 My darling wife! What is the matter, angel?
What is this saddled horse doing in my yard?

130 Where have you been, little love, at such an early hour?
That your skirts are wet with dew?
I was in the greenwood, mowing green grass,
My dearest.

131 The girls are sitting in the tower, wearing golden garlands,
The lads pass by, wearing spurs on their boots.

132 The harvest is done, the harvest is done;
Farmer, prepare us a good toast to drink.

133 Ah, let's clear out of here, for they'll come to blows!
Let's not go till the violins are playing.
Bring wine for the Magyar, brandy for the Slovak,
Beer for the German!

134 By Árokszállás there was great peril, It drove, and
drove us, and it drove us, No mercy was shown.
Its cause was a bald prince, who roared like a dragon.

135 My star, my ferryman, take me across the Danube!
I'll give you the sheepskin coat my husband left me!
I won't ferry you across, no, not I.
For there are heavy ice-floes on the Danube.
For there are heavy ice-floes on the Danube.

136 Rákóczi, Bezerényi,
Famous leaders of the Magyars,
Ah! Alas! Hungarian people,
You are withering away like flowers,
Gripped in the talons, the talons of the eagle,
You are withering away like flowers.

138 Let us renew the praises of the Apostle Saint Peter
By celebrating his feast with good cheer.
O Saint Peter, absolve us of our sins,
Ask the Lord's forgiveness for our sins.

139 No sooner, no sooner had I got married
Than I fell to grieving;
I did not love my husband,
Had him murdered by a crony of mine.

140 Hail, Treasure of Heaven,
    Holy Mother of the glorious God,
    Virgin Mary, bright Dawn of our Salvation.

141 Reap, my pet, reap,
    I will pay you your pence,
    If I don't pay them to you,
    My sweetheart will!

143a Why does he whose fortune is in ruins
    Trust in the perfidy of this world?

  b Thus, and thus, are the three young soldiers drinking
    Behind the locked door of Zsigmond Biró's wife.

  d Alas! How fast the joy of this world fades!
    How suddenly all its beauty changes!

144 At the top of the vineyard stands a pear-tree firmly planted, firmly planted;
    On one of its branches, Teréz Recika is weeping.

145 Beautifully sings the little lark
    High up in the air.
    I must go to become a soldier.
    All the girls are weeping for me.

146 It was long ago (and) will be a long time yet
    Before I again have a lover
    Whose gentle arms
    Will hug my shoulders.

147 Don't go to sleep, light of my two eyes,
    The star of rosy dawn will soon be up.

148a Let us praise the Holy Virgin, Jesus's Mother,
    Pure Gold of Heaven,
    Lovely Treasure of the sky,
    Brightest Ornament of the round world.

  b This girl weeps when she is crowned with a wreath.
    She is going to church, thinking of a maiden's lot,

She holds a rosary and small prayer-book in her hand,
Her eyes shine like two stars in the sky.

150 On the side of a high crag
Grows the cure for love.
Those who have never known love
Assert it is merely a dream.

151 Oh come, let us remember the great and miraculous
power of Eternal God
By which he brought us, old Hungarians,
from Scythia to the good land of the Magyars,
As once he led forth the Jewish people from
the hands of Pharaoh and from captivity.

152 Sad it was for me
To have been born into this world,
Since I have to suffer
Things I hoped not to know.

153 Pannonia is heading for great disaster;
As by swelling waves of the ocean,
By the flood of much trouble and sorrow it is surrounded,
For one of its heroes has perished today.

154 I am a soldier, defender of my country,
Mother is crying because they take me away,
Mother is crying and my dearest love's grieving,
A black flower of mourning laments in her window.

155 Never a farthing did I give to the church,
Whenever a beggar asked alms of me, I sent him flying.
Lute players, drummers, trumpeters made I rich,
For one false, worthless kiss I gave a hundred guineas.

156a Many are slandering me now, innocent as I am,
Let them wear out their tongues to no avail.
Jealous people attack me, they abuse me despicably,
But my God will not leave me unprotected.

   b Let them gossip and run me down—to no avail:
God will not leave me unprotected.

c A little dove with yellow feet is walking in the meadow,
  The feet are yellow, the wings green. Oh, how daintily it walks!

157 Weep, my love, as I am weeping,
    I must bid you farewell
    Let our parting be brief,
    Lest it hurt my cheerful heart,
    Lest it hurt my cheerful heart.

158 Oh, what misery is my lot!
    I have wandered about this deceitful world so long,
    I have wandered about this deceitful world so long,
    That now I am the prey of envious tongues!

159 They began to build the great castle of Déva,
    They could not raise its wall.
    What they built in the morning fell down by noon,
    What they put up at noon fell down by nightfall.

160 The grapes ripen because they are blown by many winds
    My heart breaks because it is tormented by much grief.
    He whose youth is tormented by much grief,
    Should expect no good for the rest of his life.

161 This world is full of misery for us sinners
    When we think about the days of our life,
    For we are steeped in pride,
    Woe betide us in this vale of tears!

162 The time has come for me to flee,
    To go on my wanderings,
    Many are the reasons
    For my flight.

163 Youth, like a falcon,
    Is happy so long as it is free;
    But as for my poor self,
    My heart expects no more carefree hours.

164 Do not marry a girl for her gold and silver,
    Her fine clothes, or her wreath.

Love her rather for meekness,
For her pretty gait.

165 A little duck is swimming on a black pool,
It is getting ready to join its mother in Poland.

166a I do not love, I do not love,
I do not love anyone else.
My love taught me,
Whom I shall mourn until I die.
But if ever I must live again,
Then I must be afraid of everybody,
From my own dear love
I am forced to part.

b I will never love more,
I will never love more,
A friendship taught me,
Which will grieve me till I die.
But if ever I must love again...
I want no one but you;
Life without you has turned
To painful suffering.

167 They're coming, they're coming, they're coming to fetch me;
Where is my bridal veil, I must make myself ready;
An ox-waggon is at the gate,
The bridegroom at the door,
The bride is standing at the window.

168a I don't care for Cyprus wine,
Nor for red Burgundy or Rhine wine,
The wine of Malaga,
So help me God,
Does not warm me up.

b 'Drink' is a good word, 'Pay' is not,
That is a true Hungarian saying... (there is no further text)

. . . .

c Drink, Petro, to pay is not good,
That is a true Hungarian saying,

When one has no banknotes,
One has copper coins,
Pawned is my felt-cloak,
But that's not so good.

169 Flowers of three kinds are contending for me,
My flower, I'll go with you,
My flower, I'll never leave you.

170 My garden is full of salvias,
A young couple is a lovely sight,
My pearl, my violet,
My golden apple, you.

171 My garden is full of salvias,
A young couple is a lovely sight,
My gentle violet, you,
My lovely golden apple.

172 D'you think it'll last for ever
That I'll never have a sweetheart?
Never have one! But I *have:*
Prettier and better, even, than you!
R: Hey, rose, hey!
   Hey, ho, hey!

173 Proud bride with a mouth like a little shoe,
Proud bridegroom's mouth like a moccasin.
R: Rose of my heart, rose of my soul, hey, my flower, hey!

174 Whom did you sleep with last night?
With a handsome, fair-haired boy.
R: Oh, my rose, my violet,
   Kiss both my cheeks!

175 A woman had three daughters:
Love-lorn flowers, love-lorn flowers;
There's no more precious treasure than a heart
That's never, never filled with sorrow.

178 The herd is swarming, the herd is swarming, All around
    at the bottom of the meadow.
    Oh, where shall I head them off? In the middle of a forest.

183 Miller, where's your money?
    My money's in the drawer,
    Its my life I'm anxious to save.

184 Jámbor, Faktor, come home, come home!
    Hey, hey, boom, boom, come home, come home!
    Hey, hey, boom, boom, come home, come home!

189a My heart is burning in fiery flames, believe me, for you,
    Every time I remember what we said,
    The many gay words you said to me,
    The gentle kisses you lovingly showered on my cheeks.

  c Little pied dog, what's the use of barking?
    I've a sweetheart in the town of Somlyó,
    I'll not give up my blonde for all the world,
    Nor the brunette for little Hungary!

190 A big-nosed flea, Began to make his home with us,
    For dinner, and supper, He was always present with us.

191b My boots are made of pigskin,
    My father brought them from Süke.

  c Welted top-boots, shirt with buttons,
    Nothing in my stomach.

196 God be with you, land of my birth, For all I know you may
    already be green.
    I once trod you, I am no longer treading you, God be with you,
    I am leaving you.

201 From beyond the Tisza, a herdsman lad am I. I watch over
    thirty-three sheep.
    Come, my darling, head off the leader of the flock, Lest
    it graze on curly leaves!

202 I ate porridge and burned my mouth. Who will take
   care of my mother?
   I see now I shall not, poor thing, I am leaving her
   to the care of the good Lord.

203 The rain is falling, falling gently, it wants to be spring.
   How I wish I were a tea-rose in my darling's little garden.
   I can never be a rose, I am wilting in a soldier's uniform.
   In a three-story artillery barrack in Budapest.

205 Oh two of my hens from last year, three from the year before,
   If you knew they were mine why did you feed them?
   Cluck, cluck yellow, cluck, cluck brown, cluck, cluck all three!
   My cock is not lost either, I suffered no loss.

206 Bonny swineherd what have you cooked? Lung with cabbage.
   How did you thicken it? With a side of bacon.
   And is the old man eating? Fill up his bowl!
   If he won't eat any, then fling it in his face.